Time
Marches
On

ANCHOR BOOKS
Poetry by the People for the People

First published in Great Britain in 2001 by
ANCHOR BOOKS
Remus House,
Coltsfoot Drive,
Peterborough, PE2 9JX
Telephone (01733) 898102

HB ISBN 1 85930 904 6
SB ISBN 1 85930 909 7

Foreword

For many of us the medium of poetry offers us a voice - a voice to speak out and let others know what we feel, think and desire. It is the vital bridge of communication that lets us share our innermost thoughts and messages on life to people who may need that vital surge of poetic inspiration. If offers experience to those with none or little, spreads light to those in darkness and at the same time it encourages others that they are not alone.

Time Marches On is a unique collection of poetry written in a variety of styles with the theme of past and present. The poems are easy to relate to and encouraging to read, offering engaging entertainment to their reader.

This delightful collection is sure to win your heart, making it a companion for life and perhaps even earning that favourite little spot upon your bookshelf.

Editor
Sarah Andrew

To

Sue and John

March 2002

from

Doreen

My poem on

Page 182

Contents

The Poems

Then 30s And 40s - And Now

Then five years old, free, without a care
Mother, washed and brushed my hair
Home from school, in time for tea
Mother, always there, to greet me.
Summer days, full of fun, and sun
Sunday school, home for tea
Walks in the woods, stream, picnic tea.
Father carried, when tired we be
Happy days, long ago!
Where did they go?
War, rations, air raids, worry for Mother
ARP for Dad, Army for my brother, girl guides for me.
School, gas masks, soldiers everywhere, what's for tea?
At fourteen, school was left behind, a new life began
New friends, long journeys, by bus to work
Dances, cinema, queue for everything, food, bus, ham.
Time has flown, marriage, loved ones gone
Children, loved, married, moved on
Things from childhood, long forgotten, almost
Until small things, awake your mind
And precious moments, come floating back
Birthdays, holidays, children's weddings
Homes, we've made, have come and gone alas!
Until, our three score years, are past
Sometimes I wish I was a little girl again
But years and wisdom, play their part
And love, come from the heart
And we two, will share, the life we've left
Hubby and I, and memories, kept locked there forever.

Irene G Corbett

Concern

Bugs and butterflies
Worms and moths
That as children we stepped upon
As we were running fast across the park
Down to the river
To feed the ducks

In those early years
We noticed not our accidental wrath
Nor the creatures' sad predicaments.

We were too busy
Smiling into the sunshine
Running to the squash and sandwiches.

It's only when
We come a cropper
That we notice
The poor grasshopper.

And closely consider
The little things
Even those that bite
And sting.

Simon Morton

In The Days Of Yore

I watched a film the other day
It surely chased my blues away
The 'Mark Of Zorro' was its name
Tyrone Powers' climb to fame
I love to watch the films of days gone by
They bring back memories and a sigh
For all the things that are no more
For memories from the days of yore
'Flash Gordon' oh how we shouted
Stamped our feet and some got clouted
The tupenny rush on a Saturday
Certainly chased our blues away
We had such fun when we were young
I'm sad those happy days are done

June Clare

For A Moment

The tinsel all the glitter
What is it really for
When nobody stops to mention God any more
I do love the tree mind
With lights all shiny bright
Because that makes me try to forget
Man's sad plight
Well just for a moment
Or maybe a little bit more
And then it's all back to reality
And darkness all once more.

A E Jones

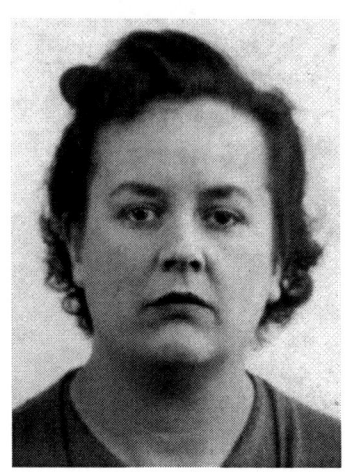

Yesterday

When I was young years ago,
You would think that life was slow
But we went fishing with jar and net,
Went with others we called our set,
Followed the lamp lighter with his pole,
Fed the horse that delivered coal.
School every day and teacher would say
When I give an order you must obey.
We went to town at weekend by tram
I bought a pot for Mum for the jam.
How quickly those years fled
Then war clouds gathered overhead.
I am sorry for the children of today,
They have forgotten how to play
They have computers and TV
But it's mostly drugs and thuggary
Scaring teachers and the law
There's no respect any more.
One wonders if and when
It will ever be now
Like it was then.

Rene Kowalski

Now And Again

Not just now and again
I take up this pen
And write, and remember again and again
All that god has blessed me with
A husband, a family, and to six children, having given birth
One severely handicapped, my first too, but then
Mine is the added blessing, of six grandchildren
Also now, amen
In my years, have come those tears, and I admit
At time deep fears
But patience, and love, have throughout all these
Years, been my stay
And even though, my health did prove a problem
Sometimes, and a burden to their day
It was on these occasions, I simply, learned to pray
I could sing, I loved to hear music, and in my home
Life, it surely did bring, some light relief
Sorrow has taught us, joy, life has brought us
And now as a grandma, my energy does zing
I still can sing, and to my grandchildren also
Now bring, a laugh, some joy, a smile
My faith express too, as some awards I have won to
Be true, in doing just that, all the while
All part it has been, and of our Christian life
And not just, a now and then fact of life, to but here
Compile

M Lightbody

State Of Mind

What was is gone
What is, is new
Some say for the better
But what I knew
And what I know
Just don't seem to differ.

Maxwell Anderson

Now And Then

'Come and have a drink,' they say, 'six o'clock on Wednesday'
I hold my glass, I have to shout, what can that be all about?
Was it gossip that I heard? I hardly caught a single word
Something about Mary Brown, but of her the noise did drown,
My host and hostess are so kind, to thank them soon I have in mind
Little tasty bits to eat - certainly a gourmet's treat
The more they drink, the more the noise
Some of them are only boys.
My ears are ringing, time to go and say 'I have enjoyed it so.'

Parties in the days gone by - they were fun, I'll tell you why
Something that we all enjoy, no more shouting to annoy
Games we played were really fun,
Something good for everyone.
Pin a name upon your back - someone famous or just Jack?
Hunting for a hidden clue. I can't find the thing can you?

Play charades to guess a word that no one here has ever heard
Pin a tail upon a donkey everyone has got it wonky
Light a candle sitting on a rolling pin. It's quite a con
Most of us are on the floor
But Jim has a surprise in store.
He's sitting there, the candle lit
It didn't worry him a bit.
Supper next in buffet style, sit and chatter all the while
Gentlemen are at your side, a snack or glass of wine provide
For our host and hostess praise
Give me back the good old days.

Joan Last

My Unknown Gift

One day while visiting my gran,
I saw a box upon the shelf.
With being the first time that I noticed,
I was curious to know, just what it was.
To ask Gran to explain, I was wasting both our time.
She never would reveal, told me one day, it would be mine.
When I was in that room, and wanted to have a peep,
Someone entered in that room,
Whenever I got near.
As the years rolled by, and I was growing up,
In my thoughts, I was always wondering,
Whatever was in that box.
That day when my gran passed away, it became my property.
Someone took it from the shelf, and handed it to me.
As I slowly lifted up the lid, and had a peep inside,
There was the ring, I'd dreamt about ever since I was a child.

Joan Craven

Now And Then

Then I was younger
By fifteen years.
My heart sing a song
As I relive this time
Sea sand and sun
Was lavishing me with fun
Now I am older
And feeble at times.
My spirits though
Are on a cloud
For I am flying all the time.

Carolie Pemberton

The Fair

Each pre-war spring the fair came to this field,
'Old Nobby Bramley's field' we called it, where
He kept his pigs, on fair-days well concealed!
From home across the road I'd stand and stare.

The day the fair was due, excitement grew;
We listened for the chuff and clank, to hear
First showman's engine with its lengthy queue
Of heavy-laden trailers was quite near.
It made tight turn to seek approach more straight,
- We watched the engine-driver's skill, wide-eyed -
As steaming monster squeezed through narrow gate
With scarce a foot to spare on either side.

The field is quickly ringed with caravans;
Once more the brothers Walls have brought their skills
(Twins had wed twins! Unique in Fairground clans?)
To give us village folk both spills and thrills.

Men empty vans of gaudy beasts and gear
For carousel, prancing steed, strutting cock.
Switchback, dodgems, swings, chair-o-planes appear
As, mushroom-like, rides grow against the clock.

Night falls; steam up, the flywheels turn, lights blaze;
Dutch organ grinds out marches, tunes from shows;
The rides stir into life through smoky haze.
We youngsters are the first to 'have our goes'.
We shot on range, our pennies rolled, we tried
Our strength, ate candyfloss and challenged fear.
'Lord Nelson', 'Dreadnought', and 'The Nation's Pride'
Steamed power for all. (No smelly diesels here!)

I'd lie awake to hear the Anthem played,
The engines die, and watch the last lights fade.

Geoffrey Matthews

If Pendle Could Talk

Did they really work their spells, Chattox and Demdike?
Would we today be just as scared as folk on misty nights?
Who heard the mutterings around Malkin Tower,
And was Alice Nutter possessed with evil powers?
Today we laugh it off but in King James the first's time
Eerie, unusual happenings were thought a witch's crime
We view Pendle fresh and green in summer's day,
At eventide it can look so different dark and grey.
History records vengeance, suffering and death,
Oh! What a tale could be told if Pendle had breath.

Mavis Catlow

Miracles Do Happen!

I used to go to St Margaret's school,
And I left when I was fourteen years old.
I could not go to work, as you will see
When this story has been told.
My mum had a hole in her heart, and she was very ill,
My dad was a sawyer, and he worked at a wood mill.
My mum brought me into this world,
So for her I wanted to do my best,
To try and make her well again, and give her a complete rest.
The doctor said she would never be able to work again,
But I wanted to prove his words were all in vain.
Dad used to get up at 5.30am, he had to be at work
At 7.30 in the morning,
He used to light the fire to get the kettle boiling
And have his breakfast in the dawning.
My brother Albert worked at the coachworks
Serving his apprenticeship,
Sisters Flowie and Ethel were at school, so off they would trip.
I used to get Mum downstairs and sit her in an armchair,
Then I would give her a wash and comb her hair.
I would give her some breakfast and prepare a meal,
Then I would dress her which was quite an ordeal.
Mum used to teach me to cook and make a beef pudding for the family,
It had to be in an iron saucepan on top of the stove you see,
It was the only stove we had, with an oven on both sides,
It had to be cleaned with black polish to make it shine.
All the saucepans and kettles had to boil on the top as well,
It was hard work to clean, and the fire going as well.
We only had one cold tap and a copper to light when we had a bath,
In front of the fire was a fender and I had to whiten the hearth.
All the family would come home to dinner which was a rush for me,
I would pop in a rice pudding to come in for their tea.
After I washed up I would take Mum out in a wicker bath chair,
We used to hire it every week, it did Mum good to get some fresh air.

It was hard work to push it Mum had to steer the wheel
In front of the chair,
I used to take her to see her sister and have a cake

And a cup of tea there.
Then up the hill to push her home, then give the family their tea,
That is how I met Bert watching me go past his works you see.
I never knew at the time he was watching me, it came in the later years,
When I was able to go to work then our romance started there.
When I look back I wonder how I coped with all that work,
But my one desire was to make Mum well again and never did I shirk.
There was no switches like today to cook and make a cup of tea,
No wireless, TV or cleaner, washing and polishing floors that was me,
But they used to shine and make my work seem worthwhile.
With a cosy hearth rug in front of the fire added a bit of style.
I would make some bengess food with a glass of wincanes
To give Mum some strength,
With her willpower and perseverance she began to feel content.
Mum began to get stronger as months and years went by,
It gave me hope and seemed like a miracle and worth my good try.
All the family were pleased and God answered my prayers you see,
When Mum was able to work, and share looking after the family with me.
Dad didn't earn much money, and he had doctors' bills to pay,
So he couldn't give me much money for looking after the family every day.
When I was sixteen Mum was well enough for me to get a job,
I worked at a holiday camp as a waitress to earn a few bob.
Bert used to come and meet me and take me home at night,
I enjoyed working there, the job for me seemed just right.
One night Bert came to meet me and said Mum had a little girl,
I could not get home quick enough, I felt all in a whirl.
It was my sister Doris born that night, so the doctors were wrong and I was right.
Two and a half years later, Mum had twins but sadly one was dead.

The lovely little girl Jean lived for three years
Till diphtheria took her away just after I was wed,
Mum used to be with all the grandchildren when they were born,
She was with me when I had David one morn,
Then she helped to bring Carol into the world
Everyone was pleased I had a lovely little girl.
Mum used to do paper hanging and dressmaking as well,
So you must never give up hope when sickness makes you unwell,
Miracles do happen you see now this story has been told,
And I am proud what I did as Mum had a heart of gold.

Olive Peck

Now And Then . . . (No 1)

Now and then
  Mine heart, and head - so sore:
Troubled by this and by that . . .
  Friendless, and so very poor
And yet,
  Christ loves me
Not just now, and then
But, forevermore . . .

Then, and now -
  Tho' that don't make sense!
For now may never, become then!
  For He's, always, in the present tense
In spite of the worries of men -
  Our feeble, woeful brows . . .

Now and then
  I feel like giving up!
So much trouble, sent!
  (Must look after myself):
For, most shall pass me by
  And, I can't rely on men
But, rather, keep on lookin' up
  For help that's heaven-sent,
Tho' men would have me on the shelf,
  Turning from the tears I cry . . .

Back then· When I didn't know Him -
  Sure 'nuff, I lived in the now . . .
But now, I know I know Him
  And tho' this troubled brow
Bends and breaks, with the strain,
  Nowt shall ever match (His) pain . . .

Anon

The Witch

They say she was a witch I say that was right,
But white not black unless you want a fight,
With a black widow on her cheek,
And no man in her bed every night,
Men would try and concur for their ego,
And then they would feel her bite,
Would you like to try your luck?
She might put her spell on you,
Weave her web and eat you up,
Spit you out when she has had enough,
She can make you feel high to fly is so good,
But only the chosen few,
Because she is after a fly for her spider to catch,
Now she flew away from you,
But empty inside searching for her pride,
Will she ever be satisfied?
Silver lady now I am untouchable for just any man,
Must be special for my brew,
To make me feel high for my bird to fly,
I cannot believe there's one like you,
So if you're just out for fun beware be on the run,
Don't play games with this witch,
Because you only get what you give,
And when I give it all next time not to fall,
Special person no tricks,
I want to love and be free with someone close to me,
That's not frightened of the talk,
So if you fill that gap I'll let you scratch my back,
And lover you have it all.

Anne Joyce Farley

Lost In Limbo

A word, a thought, a memory,
comes flashing back,
then forever lost in my mind.

A touch, a smell, a taste,
comes flooding back,
then forever lost in my mind.

A sweet embrace,
a tender kiss these,
I feel are real today,
then forever lost in my mind.

Turn on the kettle, switch on the gas,
how do I make tea?
Who is that man following me?
then forever lost in my mind.

Why is that man in my house
watching my TV?
calls me May, oh never mind,
then forever lost in my mind.

He smiles at me at me so tenderly,
I smile back, I remember him,
I think! Flashes of a wedding ring,
then forever lost in my mind,

Grope for the light in the dark,
this isn't my house,
I must hang the washing out,
then forever lost in my mind.

Lost in limbo nothing makes sense,
I lie down to die,
he's here again, that man
holding my hand,
then forever lost in my mind.

Kath Gabbitas

Christmas Eve

Celebrations and joy that
Christmas brings
I turned to the phone
as it rings
dropping the receiver on the floor
didn't want to listen to
that voice no more
She tells me you have
Gone
it was for the best
God's taken his hand
he needs to rest
I listen to choir as they
Are singing
the happiness and gifts
that Christmas is bringing
just tears and sadness
that's what I receive
I'll never forget that Christmas Eve.

Kathy Johnson

Remembering

I can remember my childhood days,
It seemed forever summer, in a beautiful blue haze.
There was happiness that would always last,
Carefree years of wonderful holidays,
Which were always by the sea.
Even my schooldays were filled with fun,
Learning wasn't always easy,
But it had to be done!
Now in my twilight years I'll quite often reminisce,
And remember those far off wonderful times,
That will live in my memory all of my days.

Val Bermingham

Then And Now

In summer time when soft winds blow
And happy laughter fills the air
When farmers start to reap and mow
'Tis time to cast away dull care

'Twas then I sought the countryside
To stretch my legs and fill my lungs
Go gaily forth with sprightly stride
Seeking solitude and sweet birds' songs

O'er Worcestershire's fields and rolling hills
O'er Stafford's moors and Cannock chase
Long had I roamed and pleasures filled
As I went my way at leisured pace

Such were the pastimes of my youth
Oft shared with family and with friends
Now aged I face another truth
As years go by such pleasure ends

I can no longer leap and bound
Cross rocky streams o'er gates and stiles
Still I live contented as now I've found
New ways that passing hours beguile

Take this advice - new pastures seek
Get up and go don't just sit there and mope
Lest you should become an old aged freak
You'll be surprised to know - how well you cope

H H Steventon

Here's To Life

Life's tragedies,
Done and dusted,
Reduced to numbered tears left in the hearts of those who cared.

Life's lessons,
Mistakes over with,
After the cause lived with the effect for a lifetime of pain and regret.

Life's friends,
Left behind,
But not forgotten
At least by those who share the memories.

Life's tears, buried deeply,
Locked away in the hearts of those who suffered.
But who now lay sleeping, as white as a sheet,
Drained of blood
And kissed by the cold blue lips of death,
As if run through by sharp ice.

Life's surprises.
Those many shocks, sending spasmodic electrical impulses
down the spine,
Shattering nerves like glass,
Twitching limbs like those of a freshly slaughtered pig.

All the while life
Trickles away,
Soaking into the earth,
Ready to breed new life.

Tegan Locke

Evacuation

As hand in hand we stood there in that miserable school hall,
My sister tried to comfort me when I began to bawl,
I was four, she was five, evacuated to stay alive,
Away from bombs and dangers, sent to live with strangers

Chosen by a cruel pair, we soon knew nothing but despair,
Beaten for things that had been done by that dreadful couple's only son.
We took the blame, cooped up in that house of shame.
Unwanted, neglected, never loved
How we prayed we would be moved
Back to danger, far away from strangers

Far too long we suffered through that sad, sadistic pair
I still recall the pains I felt
When beaten with that leather belt.
I shed so many silent tears for Mam and Dad throughout the years

But that was many years ago, I've lived to tell the story
I look at all my grandchildren and life in all its glory
And pray that no more children have to face that situation
From now on I can look at life as one big celebration.

June Plange

Happy OAP

We never dream, when we are young,
the day will come, when we're not so strong,
glasses to make things more clear,
a hearing aid to help us hear,
a stick to help us plod along, being told *'Oh no* you're wrong;
clicking knees and aching back, pills for vitamins we lack
a jar to put your dentures in,
softening cream for wrinkly skin
embrocation, for ageing bones,
no longer eligible for loans,
> but take all this, with a daily laugh
> and stop and look and see
> there's plenty going on all round,
> for the happy OAP.

Jacqueline Claire Davies

Going Home

I took the back way home,
The quiet way.
Leaving the noisy road behind,
The roaring buses, speeding cars,
The cyclists weaving in and out,
I turned aside
Into the quiet lane.

The tumult dimmed, dissolved.
The quiet lane
Was draped with shady trees and cool.
I wandered slowly, savouring
The peace, the bird-song sweet and clear.
The quiet way,
Though longer, led me home.

Now in my later years
The quiet way
Sees many others, old as I.
Finished with life's tempestuous pace,
Work's daily stress and feverish haste,
In peace we walk, in step with Christ.
The homeward way
Is rough - yet firm and good.

And younger feet now find
The quiet way.
Just for a while they walk with me
And smiling talk - and listen too.
Young wistful eyes ask silently
'Is God still true
When old age overtakes?'

May every step of mine, each word and deed
Proclaim th' unchanging faithfulness of God!

Hazel Bradshaw

Remember Me?

I've worked with people, old and young,
those that don't and do, like having fun.
Those that don't, I can hardly recall,
those that do, seem to easily fall.

To the forefront of my mind,
which makes me wonder.
How I'm going to be thought of,
when I leave this world behind.

Will I be remembered, as old and moody?
wearing thermal pyjamas and no longer.
As my daughter so innocently puts in,
sleeping at night, in the nudey dudey.

Come to think of it, does it matter,
will I care, if I get slower and fatter?
Eventually I'll die, so it won't matter to me,
but I'd like to think, in my family history.

I'll be thought of as having had fun,
enjoying life, during rain or sun.
Remembered for the daft poems,
and short stories I've written.
and I hope people will forget the time,
I accidentally . . . microwaved a kitten!

Danny Coleman

Growing Old

Growing old is not much fun
Creaking knees no longer run.
Hands that fail to grasp the thread
No wolf whistles, no 'street cred'
Hair that once shone chestnut hue
Speckled now with grey all through,
Crows' feet dance across this face
A once lithe figure's lost its grace
Wrinkled neck, each turn a pain
I'll never lissom be again.
Inside my head I'm firm and young
The lass to whom the love song's sung.
But I can smile at time's mean jests
And through my autumn days these tests
And irksome trials I'll rise above
While I've got you to call me 'Love'.

Mair Patchett

Then And Now

I remember being five
I was very much alive

I remember being six
Bowling hoops with wooden sticks

I remember being seven
I was keen to be eleven

I remember being eight
I could jump the garden gate

I remember being nine
Walls and trees there were to climb

I remember being ten
I was very grown up then

I remember being twenty
Boyfriends - dances - there were plenty

I remember twenty-nine
Motoring travelling all the time

I remember nearing forty
Getting old and rather portly

I remember fifty sixty and lots more
All these years have opened doors

And now I've come to eighty-four
I can do these things no more
But in my old and muddled brain
These precious memories still remain

Anne Purves

To Whom It May Concern

Dear friend, how like the tide is life.
For twenty years it floods, and then
It ebbs for two score years and ten;
And with its undertow, 'Belief',
Like grains of sand, is swirled apart.
What seemed important once is not,
While other values, sieved, allot
Themselves a favoured place in heart
And mind. So, Wisdom's tale unfolds,
Revealing goodness, beauty, truth,
At first, maybe, in forms which youth
So rarely comprehends, or holds
Important in their flood-tide days.
Quite still these values lie, unseen,
Until, with age, (as life has been
Benign or gentle in her ways,
Severe, perhaps, and even hard),
They manifest what we must know
Of self, of neighbour, Nature; oh,
And God to boot, without whose Word
We truly find ourselves adrift.

Just now morale ebbs low, I fear;
The church that fails, (thought not the Faith),
Poor health which, in its aftermath,
Leaves cobwebbed thoughts, all grey and drear.
But even so, the prospects, bright,
For waves mount tides which ebb or flood.
So, till it turns, on these things brood,
Dear friend, to whom, in faith I write.

John Beazley

Wings Of My Verses

Oh freedom of wings! . . .
That you give me loving verses
Gliding from rainbows to gardens
Of my yearned-for child days

Child of horizons and birds
Bathing freely on the wind
Conquering meandering rivers
In that land of infant-hood

Boy bewildered in that ecstasy
I hear you singing and laughing
Like a playmate coming back
With amusing echoes of our past

We were good to each other! . . .
Playing to a fatiguing frenzy
Is it that you are thirsty again
Wanting to drink from my fountain?

Come close dear child, let's fly
Let's climb the wings of my verses
I'll invite you this time, to my world
. . . Soaring skies with no boundaries.

Let's conquer today's dream
. . . Adventures and meanings
Delighted like yesteryears
As was our world without fears

Hold-on, oh dear child . . .!
To the new me I've discovered
In a land of adult excitement
A land of stillness and writings

Eduardo Del-Rio Escalona

A Daisy Chain

Quietly fading in October
  the Michaelmas Daisies
reminded of their glory days
  that single year in Pleasley's

watershed garden - childhood gone
  long before - but late bloom
negative nurturing transcends
  healing God making room.

Robert D Shooter

The Years Spanned

When we were young - by love bug stung
Thro' spring time's vale we'd wander -
Where lovebirds sang on tree tops high
And two sweethearts grew fonder.
It was for us love at first sight,
Far away was our next date -
Or so it seemed in our young days
With kiss goodnight at garden gate.
Thoughts of marriage then grew stronger,
As did our love, each hour,
A budding love had blossomed forth
To bloom like passion flower.
And with the wintry evenings came
More need to be together,
So to the 'pictures' we would go -
Back row - warmth - any weather!
We oft times went to see a show,
Live performance so well staged,
And real romance we understood,
To be married, were engaged.
Soon wedding knot was duly tied -
Arm in arm we walked on air
Down Church aisle and through the lych gate
Future happiness to share.
Now in the autumn of our lives
Many years together spanned
Thro' silver clouds and golden years -
Thro' all changes - life is grand.

Marian Curtis-Jones

In My Younger Days

I'm a very respectable woman, a mother and a gran,
But I'd like to go back to the Fifties,
Re-live those times if I can.
So I'm dancing, bopping and jiving,
But only in my mind,
I can hardly lift my feet off the floor -
isn't life unkind.
I'd like to wear flared jeans again
And my psychedelic beads,
I'd put my Afghan coat on
And set off to a 'happening' near Leeds,
'Cos that's what we did in the Sixties,
We smoked Pot and burned incense as well,
But the last time I tried burning incense -
Went dizzy, tripped up, nearly fell.
I'd like to go back to the seventies,
In my knee length, platform soled boots,
And the long black coat with the fur round the hem -
That style I really did suit.
I'd find the old scarf, that I wound round my neck,
There was yards of it, and more,
But a long heavy coat and yards of scarf
Would weigh me right down to the floor.
So I think I shall stay just as I am,
A mother and a gran,
But I'd love to go back to those days long ago -
In my mind I'm certain I can.

Margaret Whitton

A Life's Summary

Much loved parents
Good relatives
A lovely sister
Kind and good.
A high school education.
Then a private secretary.
Married to W MacDonald-Murray.
Learned dressmaking and design.
A diploma.
Taught at St Martin's School of Art.
Exhibitions.
Sculpting and
Writing poetry.
Created the Garden of Millennia.
More work to be done.

M MacDonald-Murray

Now And Then

Stiletto heels and pointed toes
Bobby sox and nylon hose
Pageboy hairstyle or in a pleat
Nipped in waist dressed very neat
Matching accessories were a must
As was a good bra for a shapely bust
Vinyl Records back row at the flicks
Dancing skating these were our kicks
Jobs aplenty few on the dole
Pits nation-wide still mining coal
Now factories have closed all over the place
A computer's a must to keep in the rat race
Bingo, Lottery we have gone gambling crazy
Washing machines and Hoovers are making us lazy
Fashions have changed, casual now is the mode
Folk now, do not have a dress code
Nightclubs, winebars, takeaway meals
Foreign holidays hot on their heels
Prosperous families have a car in the drive
TV, computer and a Megadrive
Most women now go out to work
Enabling them to have their perks
Good health is now my top priority
Keep putting a wee dram of whisky in my tea

Margaret Land

Now And Then

Now it is the Devil's Age
  Proclaimed in TV press and stage
So called arts, crafts the like
  Going places on your bike!

Danger faced most every day
  On our roads or on our way!
Murder, deaths, injures all -
  Devil's work always on call!
Society trifles - state Lottery
  All Devil's work we all see

On every stage of public life
  No loyalty for man and wife
As previous years . . . Ah well
  Most in Church, chapels strife!
God's laws were read Christian life

. . . Fifty year in man and wife
Laughing children plan
  Homes with little strife
Living laws of God and man

Life was so clean . . . happily
  For our sixty years and three
Joy all say filled our land
  As our Father always planned

G S S Wilyman

Now And Then

These wives and husbands
Furnish their houses
With washing machines
And vacuum cleaners,
Lay bargain carpets
And tiled floors,
Properly propagate
Beautiful children
In chosen seasons,
Hopefully weeded
Of imperfections.

Those wives and husbands
In rented houses
Were proud of lino
And pumiced doorsteps,
Boiled their washing
In shared suds and coppers,
Bore honeymoon babies
Natural as weather
Greeted the fathers
Coming from battle
With tearful delight . . .

Is it their shadows
Under the lintels
That give me comfort
In my poor failures?

Moyra Stewart Wyllie

The Little Cornish Farm

On the farm there were twenty cows,
Six calves, ten sheep and two sows,
Twelve hens, a cock and four steers,
And a goose that had lived there for years.
Five ginger and tortoiseshell cats,
Kept down all the mice and the rats.
The animals all had names,
And the roads were really just lanes.
The tractor, an old David Brown,
Jolted over the ruts in the ground.
The cows were milked in their turn,
And the milk was piped into a churn.
Three milk machines sucked out of kilter,
The milk, cooled, then went through a filter,
The cooler looked like corrugated zink,
The filter of gauze, strained the milk to drink.
What would Europe say of all this now?
It would surely cause a hygiene row!
But nobody died, and no one was ill,
I wish this was how they did it still.

On the farm I saw the young being born,
Saw broccoli cut, harvested corn,
Bunched anemones and picked up taties,
Alongside the Symons', Williams', and Laitys'.
The men in 'kitty bags' and oiler macks,
Wrapped pittisporum in hessian sacks,
Up country they went from Penzance by train,
I know things won't be the same again!
The men worked harder, the weather was colder,
Everyone then seemed so much older!
Some things have changed for the good,
But I'd keep some of the old ways if I could.

Kate Laity

Memory

The memory is a funny thing -
It lets us down from time to time.
Just when we seek a quick recall
The system fails and that sublime
Expression goes and blank surprise
Contorts the face that once seemed wise.
We stutter, think and pause again;
Embarrassment brings its own sharp pain!
No thought will come until a flash
Of inspiration from that stash
Of information called the brain,
Brings to the moment something sane.
The problem gone until next time;
Oh age you help not with this rhyme!

Bill Goodwin

Days Gone By

He sits upon the park bench
And sees the world go by
The wear of time
Has passed his prime
He often wonders why

The values that were yesterday
That guided all his days
Were worn away
Each passing day
In so many different ways

In childhood there was order
And grown-ups held the sway
Seen not heard
The childhood word
That governed childhood days

But childhood days were happy
There was innocence and fun
Hard times, yes
But love to bless
And free to jump and run

Of course there was the mischief
Exploring, testing, trials
His basic roots
Forbidden fruits
Remembered with a smile

He sits upon the park bench
And sees the world go fast
What's gone away
Is not today
He hankers for the past

Ray Ryan

My Brother, Peter

I've got an older brother. He was six when I was born.
But when I got a little older, I was always very torn.
'Cos I'm just a girl, but I longed to be like him
And play Cowboys and Indians and all that sort of thing.

He had a mate called David, and together they would play
And they never really wanted me to tag along all day
So they told me I could play, but I'd have to do as I was told
And I'd agree and be the Indian, hollering loud and bold.

Of course, they always captured me and tied me to the tree
And they'd ride off in the sunset, and forget entirely about me.
But I was thick or something, and I didn't really care
'Cos they'd let me play, and I was happy, I was part of 'Being There'

Of course, my mum would rescue me, and call out to the boys
'She's been tied up for long enough, though I know she's there
                                                    by choice,
It's time that you untied her, it's time you set her free!'
So they'd come round to the fir trees and let me go, reluctantly.

Now many years have passed us by,
We've all gone our different ways
But when we get together
We remember far off days.

Peter's built a railway now,
(Supposedly for his grandson)
But when I visit, we both play
And it really is such great fun!

Rose Stedman

Memories Of Youth

How often they come back to haunt us,
Those old faded memories of youth,
That we try to believe were so happy,
But were they, really, in truth?

Oh the angst that we suffered in our teens
The love affairs destined to end,
How many times were our hearts broken
On route to that one life-long friend?

So I think, all in all, on reflection,
I can live without that sort of pain.
I'd rather be fat and turned fifty,
Than a slim adolescent again.

Joyce Walker

Memories Of Then And Now

Then I was a little girl
In those long sweet days of childhood,
An only child, I made up games
My lonely days to fill,
But they were happy carefree times
I can recall them still.

Two ducks called Gert and Daisy
A rabbit fat and lazy,
A cat called Sparky,
A Collie dog called Bruce,
Who rounded up the turkeys
When some of them got loose,
These were my friends,

But as I grew older, I had a best friend,
We were always together, like a pair of book ends.
Laughing and dancing, the night away,
Oh! to have some of that energy now!
We had no need of drugs, or the drinks of today,
To be young was enough, to the music we'd sway,
With many a boyfriend along the way.

Now? 'Don't remind me, in the past let me be,'
I look in the mirror, and what do I see?
That old grey haired lady,
Oh Lord! Is it me?
It's not! Oh! It can't be, 'I'm not old, no Siree,'
But it is! This is now, and it's *me!*

Isobel Laffin

Another Day

Another day a keener eye than mine
Might find, embedded in a trodden track
Or turned in mud along a furrow's line,
The ring you lost when we were walking back.
And experts' hands might clean the misshaped space
Through which your middle finger often slipped
And pin the artefact in proper place
And label it with words in antique script.
And eager eyes might read the words and move
To other objects on the glass displays,
Remark, examine, analyse, approve,
And leave with heavy thoughts of ancient days.
But none will know the way your hair was blown
That Sunday, when the world was still our own.

Nick Spencer

Family Ties

The first little inkling, could it be true?
I haven't the courage yet to tell you.
In those days no test to give me the fact,
it's a trip to the doctor, who with much tact
tells me I'm a mother with six months to go.
Now I await the right moment, all of a glow.
Will you be pleased? I'm sure that you will,
when the strangeness wears off and you can be still
and think of the wonder of having our own
little baby that from great love has grown.
Fifty years on I look back and see
that from that first growth has blossomed a tree.
Two sons we have, stalwart and fine,
seven grandchildren now keep up the line.
Now I hear there's a 'Great' well on its way,
and all from an inkling on that long ago day.

Joan Chapman

Memories Of Better Days

Oh! for the days of my long lost youth;
I think of them often, now I'm long in the tooth;
When I could sing and dance all night
And run up the stairs, flight after flight.

I could ride my bike for many a mile,
Long walks with the dog would make me smile.
I'd work in the garden till late after tea;
It was all so easy and a joy to me.

Now I'm a pensioner, the difference is woeful;
I can't dance at all and running is awful.
The dogs get a walk, but just in the park;
I'm always sat round the telly by dark.

I do my shopping with the use of a car
Because heavy bags I can't carry far.
The cleaning takes me three times as long,
But I still manage a cheerful song.

I look on the bright side, the best I am able,
Be grateful for blessings and food on the table.
I'm not in debt and I can pay my way;
I can sleep in peace at the end of my day.

It's no use hankering after my illustrious youth -
This is natural progression and that's the truth.
I've had my day as a young bit of stuff;
If I can't accept it - that's just tough!

Patricia Forsberg

Now And Then

Last April I was eighty-eight,
So four months later - that's my *'now'*;
Let's 'christen' nineteen-twenty *'then'*
And think of change with furrowed brow!

I'm told it's luck, that though it's grey
I still *now* have my 'thatch' of hair,
But luckier *then,* as I look back,
Was life at seven, without a care!

To cross the road needs courage *now* -
As when I reached three score and ten -
How easy when a horse and cart
Passed slowly by in days of *'then'!*

Indiscipline in local schools
Is often *now* a sad refrain,
But *then* 'twas scarcely ever known -
Because we didn't like the cane!

We *now* lock doors throughout the day -
To fail to lock is called a sin -
Whereas, until we went to bed,
Our friends of *then* would just walk in!

A forehead's furrows, showing *now,*
Reflect the worries one has had;
So was I *then,* in fact, the cause
Of furrowed brows on Mom and Dad?

Stan Eveson

Seasons Of Life

As I sit here in the autumn of life,
I reflect on times gone by,
Time of travel and adventure,
Times that made me cry.

Times when I would capture a pirate ship,
Or fly in World War Two,
Times when I wrestled a man-eating lion,
That had escaped from the nearest zoo.

Times in my spring time,
When nothing seemed to matter,
When I could eat all the chocolate I wanted,
And never get any fatter.

Spring turned into summer,
I could go to work all day,
Then come home, eat and quickly change,
And then out at night to play.

In your summer, you never think of autumn,
Or the winter when you may expire,
You're too busy enjoying life,
And you never seem to tire.

Autumn is like a sly old fox,
It creeps up on you unaware,
Before you know it, your summer's over,
And you have pains that were never there.

As muscle turns to flab, and my eyesight goes,
And my head is thinning not hairy,
I sometimes think of the winter of life,
And I've got to admit, that's scary.

Roy Beaman

Childhood

As a babe I lay in my mother's arms cosy, cosseted, clean.
Her eyes would smile down into mine with trust and love supreme.
As a child of three my father's arms, so strong and firm were they,
Would dance me round the room with joy and promise I'd be free.
Free to live my life and want for nothing it would seem.
Living in the country, I was; quite free to roam,
There was no fear of bogey men for everyone was known,
With friends I walked the many lanes to gather flowers there.
Gosh! the beauty of the bluebells and their scent upon the air.
For hours we'd jump the many becks and often land 'unsound'
We'd gather all the stones around and make some lovely dams
We'd walk through woods to seaside then rest our weary feet,
Then play another game of building castles on the beach.
Sometimes we'd go into the park where we could ride on swings
We'd ride up high to reach the sky just like a bird on wings.
Some friends of mine were dancers and classes did attend,
With concerts in the dark nights for us their loyal friends.
In summer we would hopscotch over lines with chalk we'd drawn
Forgotten now for other things the passing time has brought.
The winter time was also great, if we could skate on ponds,
But even sledging, sliding gave us fun along with boys.
Now skipping was an art we found, if we could pitch, patch, pepper,
While rounders gave us all a chance to strike, and run like
                                        hell for leather.
We liked the game of 'canon' too with empty tin and matches,
But when you had to miss the ball it left you all with stitches.
On Sundays we would go to church, morning, noon and night,
We'd listen to the stories and sing with all our might.
The songs we sing are different now, the world is changing too,
For on what shore will love abound for the very special few.
On looking back to childhood spent, how grateful now I feel,
That heart and mind are free to see, a happy family scene.

Beth Spinks

Workers' Playtime

When I was a callow youth,
Never dreamt of searching for the truth,
All the time busy working,
Never stopping, never shirking,
I was a workaholic,
With little time for fun or frolic,
But it took its creative toll,
And I was left without a soul,
Until somebody suggested I pick up my pen,
And start to write again,
And so I did,
That's what I bid you,
It's not too late,
To go out and change your fate.

Alan Pow

He Tried

Now I'll tell you the story of a man who couldn't win,
He worked so hard, he persevered, he fought through thick and thin
Despite his best endeavours he didn't reach the summit,
More than once he slipped right back just when he thought he'd done it.
But he tried.
When George was born - an only child - his parents had ambitions
They saw their son a great success, ensconced in high positions,
And while at school he studied well to meet their expectations
The trouble was he found it hard to pass examinations
But he tried.

When war broke out in '39 he joined up with the rest,
He had no stomach for the fight although he did his best
He learned to be a soldier and prepared himself for action,
Applied for a commission, failed selection by a fraction.
But he tried.

For forty yeas he slaved away against great competition,
With regular promotion he was fired with fresh ambition
The top jobs were within his grasp, he'd realised his potential,
His face however didn't fit - of course that was essential.
But he tried.

In later years, George tried his hand at musical composing,
He thought he'd write a hit or two, he found the work engrossing,
He sent his songs to publishers, his lyrics were quite clever,
Rejection slips came thick and fast - his name was not Lloyd Webber.
But he tried.

At last his long and happy life came to a peaceful end,
And those he left behind him really felt they'd lost a friend,
To various relations he bequeathed his small estate
He would have taken it with him, but he left it far too late
Though he tried
How he tried.

George Main

Old Age

I'm not growing old gracefully,
It's all too much for me -
I'm short of sleep and lack of puff
My legs won't move
The going's tough -
Each morn I wake
With some surprise
That I'm still here
To see sunrise!

Buck up old girl!
There's plenty worse -
You've got a roof,
You've got a purse!
Things might look black
But carry on, the postman's been,
                        and left a stack
Of catalogues and other stuff
Letters are rare, but you still have friends
Who keep in touch
And make amends
For the ones who forget
Where the rainbow ends.

Kate

Remembering The Sixties

I couldn't wait to start my job after leaving school,
a shop assistant I became, I really felt so cool.
I put on lots of make up and backcombed all my hair,
sprayed it stiff with lacquer, and didn't have a care.

With my buffon hairdo, eyeliner nice and thick,
I used a pale pink lipstick, I really looked quite sick.
But I thought I looked so brilliant, fashion was the key,
dressed in all the latest gear, for all the world to see.

The Beatles was the sound we heard, dancing, having fun,
a coach trip off to Blackpool, a weekend in the sun.
Stiletto heels were smashing, with great big pointed toes,
a massive handbag on your arm, we really liked to pose.

Flower power was a trend, to advertise world peace,
shirts of many colours, a waistcoat made of fleece.
They offered you a flower and quoted 'peace to man'
I sometimes think about them now, what a smashing plan.

Records was the thing back then, expresso coffee too,
we used to meet inside the cafe, a gathering of our crew.
Motorbikes and scooters, mods and rockers style,
a boy would send you in a whirl, just with a friendly smile.

I wore those stick out underskirts, with wire around the hem,
I couldn't sit down properly, hard handle them
Either rinsed in sugar water or starch if you were rich,
they used to stick into your legs and make you want to itch.

What a brilliant time this era was, every day was great,
looking forward to the fun, going out to meet your mate.
I loved the swinging sixties, the times and people then,
the girls are all grown up now, the boys that was, are men.

Now I have grown older, I think about time passed,
your teens are really precious years, they fly by very fast.

Betty Hattersley

The Candlesticks

A pale-blue mist had been encased
In the clear glass, at the making,
Preserved like my memory of you.
The candlesticks were yours, a gift.
How could others know of your pleasure,
Dusting, holding, admiring, setting them
Like that, for the mirror.

They have remained an icon of your pleasure,
Such a limited commodity in those austere years,
Handling them now takes me back,
It's my memory of you; only mine;
As untouchable as the blue mist.
How could they know?
How could you have known?
That a little boy watched
And understood.

Half a century has passed, you and I
Travel now in parallel worlds,
Connected by memory.
The candlesticks have their space,
And glisten when sun-kissed,
They gleam like steering rods
In the control room of my mind,
Keeping me on course.

Alex Laird

Me, Myself And Arthur

I wish I could smile for just a while
So my kids could say, Eh! I knew the day
That she curved her lips
As she took small sips
Of her gin and tonic
('Well they were probably slurrs and quite a few burps')
As after a few she felt bionic

She tried to walk so straight and tall
But she knew deep down she was gonna fall
Not from grace I hasten to add
Because any fella she could have had
It's age me dears that rots the brain
Then you've got no help against the pain
So grin and bear it if you can - cos,
You've lived your life with yin and yen

And then old Arthur starts to visit
It's really painful - int it
As my dear it's bone on bone
And your feelings for others turn to stone
You snip and snape from morn till night
And then you try to put things right
But you feel it's too late, they don't understand 'TG'
You're almost there on God's right hand
He's there to help me, I now,
I've just got to get my faith in tow
But a gin and tonic I'll have just now
Because tomorrow is another day
And I've got to get through it, OK!
So cheers everybody, have a drink on me
Because real soon, I'll be a cherry blossom tree.

Dorothy Rowe

Swealings

What I best remember is the stink,
sharp acrid pungency of the grey
grass-clouds, bitter, rank,

Scratching my throat like drying pee,
seeping into clothes like clammy fog
still vaguely stale at school next day.

But this was our spring festival,
the yearly rite, a hallowed pagan mystery,
for with the first sun-birth came swealing time

Inviting us into the contoured field
behind the dormant paper mill
when coltsfoot screwed shut tawny eyes
and leathery dock leaves flapped like
patient elephant ears,

And in the valley just below our sight
the lime-lodge quivered septic, putrid white,
an ulcer festering on a leper's corpse.

On high banks above we touched
each wild-haired tuft with flaming brands,
dead sourness of last year's grass
crackling vermilion, fading down to
crimson seas of pulsing fire
mocking the falling sun ball of red spring
through swirling skies of stinging cloud,

burning away the dross,
young impulse to destroy and re-create,
letting fresh green emerge and propagate.

We were the springtime kids, we
helped char the strangle-knots of age
in ruthless procreation.

Did we vaguely know
we were cremating our own ghosts
blackening out our own inpermenance
in wraiths of stormy grass-smoke?

John H Hope

Multi-Racial Treasure

Scotland, land of my father,
France, land of my mother,
Germany, land of my captivity,
How lucky I am to know you,
Your languages, your cultures and your peoples.

What have I gleaned of my passing along your way?
Family, friends and foes, all played their part.
You have enriched my life beyond measure.
Now that I have aged into maturity,
The thoughts and memories of a scattered past,
Like any cherished treasure, are my wealth
And keep me very young at heart.

Like the miser, I savour your richness
And abundance of life's experiences.
Unlike the miser, I dip repeatedly into the chest
To scatter around its valuable bounty.

Pray, listen carefully, my friend,
Say yes to life, no matter the cost
Accept its variety, admire its diversity!
The joys, the sorrows, all have their purpose.
Learn from life with all your heart, mind and senses.
Like a sponge, soak up every drop of knowledge,
There is always room for a little more.
One day, I'm sure, you will find, and be amazed,
A priceless jewel, the most coveted of all,
Peace of mind, wisdom and serenity.

Andrew Cox

Distant Memories

Now and then I must confess
I do remember that Lulu dress!
My first wages blown
On Lulu dresses of my very own

A time of happiness for me
Because of responsibility I was free
Full of love and hopes and dreams
Not worries and woes and Pension schemes!

Many regrets and errors made
Wrong roads taken in the game I played
The game of life can be so cruel
With tragedies and mistakes as fuel

A fuel that's burned for far too long
'If you survive it makes you strong'
Maturity brings wisdom shows the error of our ways
And yes the mistakes of earlier days

From Lulu dresses to a family - sons for me - one, two, three
Then divorce - again I am free!

But the wisdom I have gained now has come too late
For I did make so many mistakes
Now there is time to reflect
And life is filled with regret

We do what we think right at the time
How I wish those dresses were still mine!

Tricia Layton

Chasing Rainbows

We spend our lives chasing rainbows,
ever elusive, evading our grasp.
Strive how we will, it's an impossible task.
For happiness is nearer than we know;
the power lies within us although,
it might not show.
No one, no thing, can happiness bring.
We make or break our own.
It is in *how* we deal with what life brings us,
that will achieve the ultimate goal.
Lift up your head high. Square your shoulders.
Don't hide in a hole!
A rainbow will dazzle your eyes -
it is beautiful to behold.
it is just a dream - so be wise.
Look within you. There lies the gold!

Fuchsia Coles

Old Or New?

Who would change - would want to be young?
and change your age for youth -
- would it scare you to be new to life
and make you feel uncouth?

There's so much you'd have to try and forget,
like rationing, gas mantles and coal,
real poverty and unlocked doors,
things really hard to thole.

You'll have to forget the family thing
'cos that's the way you're heading,
don't bother, you'll meet them all
at the very next funeral or wedding.

The clothes you wear bear someone's name,
this creates a great impression,
you never wear clothes that are handed down,
now, you've learned another lesson!

You must forget how to count or spell
well, at least without a machine,
do you really need that knowledge,
to live a life serene?

Now, would you change, my ageing friends?
Could you change your life about?
Will you leave the future to the young
and just sit this one out?

A Dickie

Time Passes

Some four-years-old I must have been,
　The place was Sutton-on-Sea.
Hard to believe that chubby tot
　Was ever really me!
The year, I think, was 1912,
　Two years before 'The War',
A stable world for such as we,
　Though soon to be no more.

I gathered shells upon the sand.
　Two buckets I would use,
The first to wash, the next to rinse,
　Before the best I'd choose.
A paddle, and a donkey ride
　Were highlights of our play.
The grey North Sea before us stretched
　On yearly holiday.

Two major wars, a lifetime's growth
　Divide that time from me.
Some eighty years of varied work,
　Changed, inexorably.
With loves, with deaths, the way is marked,
　Rainbows of joy and fears,
But step by step, I now can trace
　My path across the years.

Treasures of memory are mine,
　Joy too that friendships stay;
And still the child who washed the shells
　Is there, is me today.

Kathleen M Hatton

Now And Then

'Have you always been grey Gran?'
My grandson said to me.
'Have you always been grown up
Or were you once silly?'

I looked at him lovingly,
Which he saw in my eyes.
'Did I say something wrong, Gran?'
He looked up to the skies.

'I once was young and pretty.
I once was really slim.
I once had a well-paid job
Working with Grandad Jim.

I worked in a fine office.
I drove a modern car.
My clothes were quite expensive.
But I wasn't a star.

Until I fell in love one day
With your dear Grandad Jim.
And then I gave it all up
And went and married him.

We lived in a small cottage.
That was when life started.
And lived there 'til last April
That's when he departed.

I need to start a new life
Living without him now.
No one wants a grey old gran
In these offices now.'

'But I could live with you Gran.
Then I could be your young man.'

Catherine Craft

To My Parents

Hearts beat at the sound
Of itchy limbs
That ceaseless search
For a partner.

A man and a woman
In one flight
From drudgery
It's summer this Saturday night.

Their feet in a frenzy
Sweet and nimble
They thread their steps
Round a dance hall.

Where else will they travel?
It's the fifties
Tomorrow church
And Monday slavery.

Marylène Walker

Re-Encounters

In the shrubbery you searched
for a ball,
you with your child,
you who were once my child.

In the dim light
your image seemed to change
till it became as mine
when there I searched with you.

The wheel completes its turn;
the next I may not see
nor yet hear the laughter
when your grown child with his

Seeks for that same elusive toy.

Louise Rogers

Memories On St Valentine's Day

I look at my valentine cards of long ago
And remember the young men who gave them to me
They were so shy that passed me by
Not like today with their forward ways.

I look at my valentine cards of sweetness and hope
And remember the dance where I was given a rose
I felt the gentle touch of a hand on mine
It seemed like magic in those faraway times.

I look at my valentine cards kept fresh just like new
And wonder if the young men are old men today
Or do they watch me now, as their cards I hold?
In spirit form maybe they smile . . . to see me so old,
Now there is nobody to send me a card or a rose.

I look at my valentine cards of long ago
And hear music playing and see people dancing
Then I step forward to join them . . .
In a blue dress and my hair long and blonde.

Someone will find me sitting alone
Valentine cards on my lap, a smile on my lips
In death's icy grip they will find me . . .
Yet . . . I dance with the young man that gave
me the rose.

Jennifer M Trodd

Time, Immemorial Of History

Time wait not for us,
Carried in the waves of the sea,
Time wait not for me,
Amidst the autumn's crown of yield,
Or winter's cruel jest.
Oh little lamb of new-born faith,
Wait not for me, snuggled to your mother's snowy body.
Time, in the crimson setting sun of earth's great shield,
Spill not the blood of my rosebuds in spring,
And when the great summer bids us sing,
Time cease forever, in the resurrection of our chorales.
Come thy great giant time,
Let me pluck the great bards, from your great ancient feet,
And in the pleasures of the great bridal suite,
Let us hold each other in erotic friendship of the deep.

Elizabeth Rose French

Village Life

Children calling out with glee,
Running home from school for tea,
Past the pub down by the green,
Where the old folk sit and dream,
Chattering of the days gone by,
Under a sunny summer sky.

When village life was calm and slow,
Seems so very long ago,
Father working in the fields,
Mum at home preparing meals,
So different to today's hi-tech,
No wonder folks are total wrecks.

Never got a minute to spare,
To show the oldies that they care,
Munching meals upon their knee,
Eyes glued to the God TV,
Then rushing on upon their way,
Never stopping day by day.

G W Bailey

Dreams There Are . . .

Dreams there are, that thread the looms of time,
That hold time's lines in play,
The Master Weaver's patterns caught
Are still 'on line' today.

Dreams there are, which never change from age to age,
The actors playing follies still
Just move from stage to stage.

Dreams there are, which keep repeating life,
Birth's blueprint carbons,
Stencils through, repeating needless strife.

Dreams there are, which taken at their flood,
Show the Master Weaver's patterns wrought
Woven through His Precious Blood.

Dreams there are, that thread the looms of time,
That make time's lines still sway,
The Master Weaver's patterns sought
Are but a strand away.

Graham K A Walker

Do Something

Old, elderly, aged
Crotchety, infirm, when you're over 65
These are words you'll learn.
With which you will be labelled
Like it or not
You'll be put to pasture,
left to sit and rot,
So do something about it
Strike while the iron is hot
Give yourself an interest
It need not cost a lot.
Remember the old adage
You're never too old to learn
Get yourself a hobby
Afore your bridges start to burn.

Jacqueline Bellas

The Sun Shone Yesterday

When we were children, time for us lacked meaning.
We used it as a way of dividing the day.
Up at six, lunch at twelve, and tea at four.
Seven o'clock was bed, that was the end, as they say.

To declare we were carefree would not be enough.
Life was exciting and new.
Each day was a challenge with experiences to absorb.
And problems we had very few.

At Christmas it snowed and Augusts were hot.
The long summer days were always sunny.
We never took life serious.
And the side we found, was always funny.

But over the decades our minds have unfortunately matured.
Time now is so important we're always watching the clock.
Observing people from behind closed doors.
Which back then never, but now have a lock.

Christmas never sees snow anymore, but rain we have in plenty.
Respect a word that's not used as before.
Ill-health is common, in all of your friends.
And ill or not they're certainly poor.

Nevertheless as I observe, it could be the state of our age.
It snows when it can, and children still play.
Not everyone's sick, and not everyone's poor.
And believe it or not, the sun shone yesterday.

Garry Knowles

The Underdog

I sit alone among my souvenirs,
Photographs, faded beyond recognition:
My mother's hand-made rugs stained through the years
With strands plucked out by kitten after kitten.

Shopping by bus is tiring - all too true,
But far less so than travelling by train:
Arriving (always late) at Waterloo
Then suffocating in the City Drain.

No longer do I have to take down letters
From some rude boor, run errands for his wife:
Nor listen to smug sermons from my betters
On how I should or should not live my life.

Handsome young men with devastating charm
No longer cause my heart to miss a beat:
Even when young I never chanced my arm
Knowing the end would only be defeat.

Though swollen stiffened joints may cause some pain
(I hear the mantra 'What can you expect?')
I should not care to live my life again.
For now at last I'm treated with respect.

E R Low

Comparisons

Summer, always very hot and holidays so long,
Cuddly kittens, Father Christmas, always being wrong.
Apples sweet and crunchy, frilly party dress,
New potatoes, being told that adults know what's best.

Never sun, just wind and rain, no holidays in sight,
Endless hairs on carpets, more expense, and being right!
Lots of rush and worry, not a thing to wear,
Life is very hard, why don't the young ones seem to care?

Sandra J Walker

Memories - An Expansion Of Time

What is life but an expansion of time
between being born and going to the grave
A set of memories framed and shaped by those around us
Memories of special people and places in our lives
For me it conjures up many images
Images of my gran, a pink bathroom suite,
My sister and I climbing trees together
But the memories I hold most dear are of my son's birth
His first cries in the night, his first words
Taking his first steps at nine months old.
All precious to my soul
Long happy days spent in the park
With the sun magically weaving gold in his hair
Of course time marches on, we're both older now
But the memories will always be there
Like a video library within our minds
To play and rewind as we feel the need
To have those special ones close by once more
If only for a fleeting glimpse
Of the memories that fill the expansion of time
Between being born and going to the grave.

Trudi James

The Speed Of Time

Another year has just gone by
And I didn't see it go
I wonder if it's just my age
For they used to go so slow
I'm sure as we grow older
There becomes a new dimension
Must sort this out when I get time
And give it more attention
But if I give time to things like this
The time will go more fast
I wonder what's the remedy
To make tomorrow last
I try to keep an hour or two
Tucked up within my sleeve
But when I glance down at my watch
I swear my eyes deceive
For there it is
The day has gone
It's time to go to bed
But tomorrow may last longer
If I don't wake up dead.

Euphemia McKillop

Now And Then

When I was young and in my prime,
Dancing, prancing, all the time,
Up again at break of day,
Dressed then on my way.

Then prepare to work another day.
Home again, a bite to eat
Then out and about to meet the gang.
No worries then of aching feet

How did I ever keep the pace?
I often wonder why
My parents often told me
'You'll rue it by and by.'

Now I am much older
The years all seem to have fled,
At the end of every day
I can't wait to get to bed.

It seems an awful pity,
That we have to change,
Why does age weary us?
It seems so very strange.

Life has its compensations,
Dangling your grandchild on your knee,
The baby in his cradle
A wondrous thing to see.

Time to do the things you wish,
In your own slow time,
Quietly sit and reminisce,
Or take a glass of wine.

Barbara Appèl

From Toddlers To Teenagers

I'm only looking back, over the past ten years or so.
So I don't suppose to many that it seems so long ago.
But there's been a transformation in the decade that has passed,
My toddlers have turned into teenagers so fast.

My son was just an infant, still at his primary school,
Now he's off to college and he's acting super cool!
He'd just enrolled at 'Beavers' and thought it was a treat,
Now he's almost six-foot tall with size eleven feet!

My cute toddler daughter wore dresses, pink and pretty.
She's *now* a trendy teenager, whose stories are so witty.
She loved to go to nursery, where life was oh so simple,
Now there's such a problem over every spot and pimple!

My baby, *then,* was tiny and needed lots of care,
Now she's quite a tomboy and hates to brush her hair.
She enjoyed being cuddled and playing with her toys,
Now she plays footie on the field with all the boys!

I remember reading stories as they sat upon my knee,
I taught them all so many things, *Now* they know much more than me!
They listened to me reading about 'Peter Pan and Hook'.
These days 'Harry Potter' is their very favourite book!

We gathered round for 'Rainbow' and listened to nursery rhymes.
Of course their taste in music *now,* has changed with the times!
They've gone from teething and toddling and learning to tie their laces.
To football, dancing and homework and wearing dental braces.

Our home was littered with 'Duplo bricks', with bikes
and prams and more,
Now there are no toys about, but trainers block the door.
I view old photos and videos, amazed at how they've grown,
I look back sentimentally, yes the last ten years have flown!

Lynne Doyle

Under The Chestnut Tree

When I was very young, I'd go
To a tree up in the wood
Up the lane and across the stile
To find conkers if I could
Under the chestnut tree

I would pick up all I needed
Fill my pockets, then homeward bound
Across the stile and down the lane
Pleased with the booty I had found
From under the chestnut tree

And as I grew older
Each autumn time I'd go
To gather more conkers
And a stick at them I'd throw
From under the chestnut tree

Each year as I grew braver
Into her branches I would climb
With other boys all gathered there
Every autumn time
Under the chestnut tree

One year a girl came too
Brown eyes and copper-coloured hair
My young heart missed a beat
As I saw this girl so rare
Under the chestnut tree

And now I take my little lad
With brown eyes and copper-coloured hair
To find big shiny conkers
Dark brown and lying there
Under the chestnut tree.

Keith Coleman

Santa's Secrets

Then, Santa was a wizard man,
Who lived in Arctic snow.
He knew exactly what I'd plan
From clockwork train to toy Lego.

Each Christmas he'd arrive on sleigh
With tinkling bells on reindeer's head,
He'd leave my toys and be gone by day,
Silently, across the snow, to bed.

Chums at school would often boast
They'd sat on Santa's knee,
Whilst he ate a Christmas roast
Of sweet pudding and hot turkey.

Now, of course, with hair snow-white,
Santa's secrets I fully know.
Gifts I leave near tree at night,
And dream of reindeers, deep in snow.

Lloyd Mason

Yesterday

How much I miss the magic of the place
where I was born
And how I love the life I lived,
the times I'll always mourn.
My day now dawns 'traffic'
that spangled once on streams.
Machinery pounds in my head that dizzied
once with dreams.
I think about the winding lanes
The trees that burst with bloom.
And breathless nights beneath the stars
And singing to the moon.
Of tiny farms where time stood still
Where folk were true and good.
Of running barefoot through the fields
And whistling in the woods.
All this is gone now I am grown
But I still owe a debt
For here I learned the special things
I never shall forget.
Here I learned truth and honesty.
Tranquillity of mind.
Here I learned patience;
Here was love.
The art of being kind.
And as I lie at night I yearn for what is past
And toss and turn to traffic sounds
                    Then go to sleep at last.

Joan Patrickson

If I Knew Then . . . What I Know Now

Although I am happy now in the chosen life that I have,
Which incidentally took a long while to arrive,
I sometimes cannot help looking back at the now seemingly distant past,
If I said that I had no regrets, I would be fooling myself,
Why is it as you get older and wiser,
You realise the significance of choices you made along the way.

Back then when I inevitably took the easy option in a situation,
Weak strength of character let me down,
Others' needs came before my own,
Making me desperately unhappy,
When I so wanted to take the pathway,
That I believe now would have led to happiness.

I lived a life putting others before myself,
Not a bad thing, you might add,
Yet my hopes and dreams slipped through my fingers,
If only I could turn back the clock onto some past scenes,
Where sacrifice of the self led to tears,
Inevitably wasted youth cannot be recaptured.

How would I handle those propositions now,
With the knowledge that I have of how those events,
Moulded and shaped my life,
How I wish for that second chance,
If only for a week, a day, an hour,
Yet I know that the 'if only' moment cannot reappear.

It would need to be recaptured,
With the knowledge of foresight that I now hold,
Yet in the body of youth that was then,
A glimpse into what may have been,
Had I made different choices,
I wish, but the outcome I will never know.

Ann G Wallace

Twilight Years

You are old, Father Matthew, the young priest said,
And your hair has become very white,
Yet you ride that old bike when you go on your rounds:
Do you think at your age it is right?

In my youth, answered Matthew, I owned an MG,
And drove my parishioners crazy,
With the roar of its engine, the screech of its brakes,
And the fact that it made me so lazy.

You are old, said the youngster - your body is frail,
And your muscles can't grow any bigger.
Yet you do sponsored walks, in the snow and the hail:
Pray, how do you manage such vigour?

When I was a youngster, I used to go scrumping,
And run off with apples and pears,
And the farmer would chase me to give me a thumping,
But all he could give me were glares.

You are old, the young priest said, your voice is so weak,
And your singing is low-pitched and gruff,
But your sermons are pow'rful whenever you speak:
Pray, how d'you come out with such stuff?

In my youth, said his colleague, I sang like a bird,
And all the girls swooned at my singing.
They called me a genius, the best ever heard -
And I had to escape from their clinging.

You are old, Father Matthew, and weak at the knees,
Your face is all wrinkled and pasty,
Yet woman adore you, surround you like bees:
Why is it they find you so tasty?

Enough of this nonsense - shut up, and stand back!
Your questions are making me late!
I've got to get ready, to meet Cilla Black,
It's tonight I appear on 'Blind Date'.

K Brown

Conversation With An Old Photograph

Look at you, a wide-eyed innocent
fifteen stressful years past;
time consumed coping with indolent
bosses blown out with the ballast.

You were lost back then, too mesmerised
by the tangled trappings
of the nine to five syndrome, excised
from the dreams you screened as lapping
of young breakers refreshed your soul -
back where and when we were whole.

Forty was but a number to you,
a century away;
evil something one first invited,
before it could install dismay.

We could not imagine how a heart
might be torn from its roots
by cynical, yet still remain part
of a body leaking hope . . . mute!
Betrayal played a starring role
since days we were one and whole!

Perry McDaid

Bright Morning

A child stands there, on the still dewy grass.
Morning is his, the whole world new and bright;
Pale skies reflected in calm seas, like glass,
Deep, gleaming, in the glorious dawn of light.

The tide has left wet sand and rippled pool.
Clear, bubbling streams past silvery pebbles run.
The caves are waiting, shadowy and cool;
The sea's edge warmed and rainbowed by the sun.

High cliffs are thick with heather's honeyed bells;
The fresh grass scattered with light, starry flowers.
Faint sounds of water weave enchanted spells,
And dewdrops fall in tiny, sparkling showers.

The roses cast soft petals on the air,
Sweet-scented breath of summer days to be,
As gentle breezes wander everywhere
Bringing a salty perfume from the sea.

This world will fade. But now no shadow falls
Across the purple moor and sea's green streams.
The glory of the sunlit morning calls;
Come out into the dazzling world of dreams.

Diana Momber

Memories

Where have all the young years gone?
How quickly they've passed by.
It doesn't seem so long ago,
When I was young and shy.

Here I am with George my beau,
The man I later wed,
But life was oh! So innocent!
So often we have said.

We married one day in the month of June,
The sun shone all day long.
But that was fifty years ago,
It doesn't seem that long.

Two children of our own we had,
They in turn produced seven,
We've had our ups and downs of course,
But life was close to heaven.

Well, now we are in retirement,
But are we? I'm not so sure.
We've had some wonderful holidays
And hope to have some more.

Our leisure time? What time is that?
We're always on the go.
Dancing, walking, meeting friends.
No time to do things slow.

But of course we have been so very blessed,
With good health as we've travelled life's path.
And with God's help may it continue to be
Until we're Home at last.

E Timmins

Opened Eyes, But Unsure As To Why

I fear that my young eyes have disappeared
Replaced by scepticism and mistrust
I thought the world was fine and fair
Now I see that some don't care
I was taught to consider others and share
Why now when I give, do I feel I'm caught in a snare.
There'll be a snag and a catch
Lost because it was fixed that match
Strike a match and see its flame
If I was to blame I'd feel such shame
I continue to place my trust in others
Although when I was a child
I never asked why.

John Beals

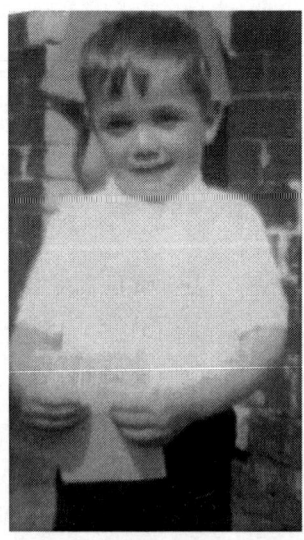

Looking Back

Looking back to yesterday, through changes that we knew
Good and bad times, through happiness and tears
But smiles would win, they always do
We counted days to summer, when holidays were near.

Looking back to days when cares were put away
Getting through the sad times as we moved along
Feeling young and carefree, tomorrow had to wait
When we were young and danced all night till dawn.

Thinking that first kiss was the best of all
Believing first love would last, dreaming all in vain
Then moving on in our youth, that's life, after all
And then to fall in love all over again.

Dreams were needed, although they never came true
But smiles took over, with disappointments fading
Crazy schemes and plans were the things of youth
When long summer days and nights were never-ending.

Looking back to yesterdays, memories linger on
Friendships and loved ones we miss
Are always here, have never really gone
Golden days to treasure, our memories to relive.

Sheila Revell

Cara Mia

As Mantovani quivered,
As Mau Mau victims bled,
You tried to wear stilettos,
I tried to be a Ted.

When Doris Day bang-jangled,
When Johnnie Ray c-cried,
I told you that I loved you,
You told me that I lied.

As Winnie Atwell tinkled
My mind was in a whirl,
Straight after Evening Worship,
You naughty Baptist girl!

When Daz was boiling whitest,
When Toscanini quit,
You had a fling with Malcolm,
I had a jealous fit.

As Billy Graham ranted
I almost lost my soul,
You came to Ely Racecourse,
I scored the winning goal.

Then youth was at the tiller,
Then youth was in its prime,
Now youth is lost forever
In the wilderness of time.

Peter Davies

Young In Heart

Where are the days of delicious anticipation -
The intensity of living,
The impatience of longing of hopes unfulfilled?
The pace slows down and we become apathetic,
Because compromise has had to be made.

But the memories are there . . .
Still strangely tender,
The wonder and curiosity
About Life and Creation,
Tempered by the years' experience:
This is a more satisfying state than Youth,
Which is all experiment and error,
Now there is firm ground beneath one's feet
On which to base trust in others,
And confidence in one's own abilities.

Life is progressive . . . there can be no going back -
Anyway, who wants to? Not I!
Surely, the greatest adventure is to come -
The emerging from this constricting physical shell
Into the awareness of a new spiritual experience!

Olive Miller

Now And Then

Oh foolish years
of youth
believing . . .
there is Time
to do
stretching
an age between
December and December
each minute a year
unending

Oh foolish years
of age
wishing . . .
there was Time
to recapture
fading
dreams of youth
when Decembers merge
each year a minute
no Time between

For never was there Time
to lose

Time
        man's measurement
                in Space

of Youth and Age
Life and Death

a veiled illusion.

Anita Richards

Once I Was . . .

Once I was tall with hair rich brown, all piled in curls on my crown
Big blue eyes alive and flashing, thought by most to be quite smashing
Once I was slim with clothes so tight, that every curve was well in sight
Once I wore skirts that were so short, quite indecent my mother thought
My heels were high my necklines low, putting all I had on show
Once athletic you will find, I left the others well behind
Whilst on the track or swimming through always finishing one or two
All that now in bygone days, as I sit here in a sort of haze
I came upstairs to get . . . but what, yet again I have forgot!
I've also shrunk now not so tall, not one brown hair is left at all
Gone are the curls from off my head, rich browns replaced
by grey instead
No longer slim in truth it's that, I really am now short and fat
No longer heels to walk the lanes, long-legged trousers hide the veins
Dark high-necked jumpers are now in, to cover up this double chin
If I sound doleful it's just because I'm thinking of what once I was . . .

Jackie Davies

It Seems Like Only Yesterday

It seems like only yesterday
That you were oh so young,
A baby in your mother's arms
Your life had just begun.

The scent of talc and baby oil
Bathtimes, mealtimes, peaceful sleep,
Baby days and baby nights
These are the times to keep.

Those pre-school days were to be treasured
All too soon they passed away,
Then came school, to you it beckoned,
Took your baby days away.

Wedding bells and marriage vows
Photographs that on display,
Align with others on the shelf
In cardboard frames from yesterday.

Come the day you both are parents
Holding in your warm embrace,
A child so frail, so small, dependant
Adoring looks upon your face.

As I watch you, quiet, unnoticed
Thoughts and memories in my mind I view,
It seems like only yesterday
In that same way I once held you.

Fleeting days of childhood ways
It seems like only yesterday,
A baby in your mother's arms
No more than just a thought away.

W D Stanley

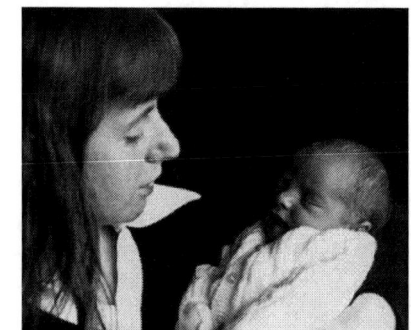

Fate

I was pretty as a girl
Blonde hair, blue eyes, and slim
Went out every night to dance
Boys, kisses - then I met Him!

The Dream, the only one for me,
We married that same year
A boy was born, another, too,
Then suddenly - 'you're not here'.

All alone with my two boys,
Back home to Mum I went.
Back to college, got a job,
Then a home again - heaven-sent.

One boy died, the other grew,
Married, had a child,
Now I reflect on my past life
Just why was it so wild?

I never saw my love again
Nor married, tho' he did . . .
I contemplate the turn of fate
Which decreed my solitude

For, devastated, I reviewed my life -
What chance of happiness now?
So I settled for solitude, no men,
To not get hurt somehow.

With many cats I spend my days
Happy lives for them, you see,
For giving happiness to them
Gives back happiness to me.

Diana Price

Remains

I used to run,
I used to skip,
but lately when I walk I trip.

I used to dance
the night away,
but I can hardly walk today.

No more the strength
I had before;
my hearing's bad, my sight is poor.

My youth has gone,
all that remains
are aches and wrinkles and varicose veins.

The times that we,
er, you know what,
well, nowadays, we'd rather not.

But I don't care
for now I find
I much prefer to use my mind.

I let my heart
control my head,
now prudence tends to rule instead.

Though youth has gone
I'm quite content
with memories of the life I've spent.

And now I have
the time to be
with those I love and who love me.

Hilary J Cairns

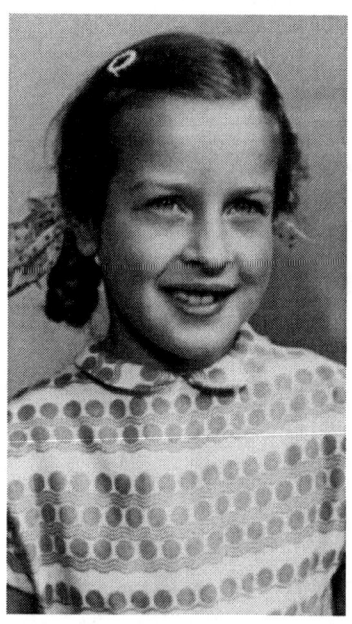

The Oak Tree

As a lad he'd climbed this tree
And dreamed his dreams of what he'd be
A train driver, a man of cloth,
(He'd laughed and then dismissed them both)
Perhaps a soldier off to war,
Or a hunter trailing a lion's spoor?
No, a sailor is what he'd be
And sail the wondrous Seven Seas.
And so he dreamed of all he'd see,
Sitting in that great oak tree.
As man and boy, he'd stood beneath
Its autumn, spring and summer leaf
It had sheltered him from rain and storm
And cooled him when it was too warm.
Picnickers ate beneath her shade,
Like a giant umbrella especially made.
With his lover he'd carved upon the trunk
A heart, when they were newly drunk
With love and hope, their hearts ablaze,
Beneath the tree in the summer's haze.

Now his grandchildren climb the tree
And dream their dreams of what they'll be
Sitting in the old oak tree.

Joan A Thomas

From Picnic To Fancy Dress

I can remember things of my younger days
from picnic to fancy dress

Hallowe'en and pumpkin pie, apple bobbing
and a twinkle in your mother's eye

Eye shadow and pretty dress and your
bedroom looking a mess

Birthday party, fizzy pop and all them twirling
games that had to stop.

Learning all your sums and cocktail bubbles
out of the blues.

Your first bicycle ride to swinging on your
swing which made your heart sing.

Jay

Reminisce

walking, walking over hill and dale
down the lanes and road we trail
footpaths tracks and leafy dells
we sit and rest in thoughtfulness
eat and drink and then move on
we stop and talk to all and one
bid a good day and then trudge away
we dream the dreams of bygone days
of horses and carts and drystone walls
of cows and sheep with lambs jumping about
birds in the hedgerow making noise and nests
foxes and badgers playing about at dusk
naughty weasels spying on all of us
and then we rest at a country inn
for a pint of ale and to reminisce
then we trudge on home
to supper and bed
and dreams of exploits long ago.

Donald Jay

Maturity

When 'teenager years' are long forgot
And 'mortgage loans' repaid,
And the memory of those struggling years
Now begin to fade.
When you no longer have that pang of guilt
As you give yourself a treat
And you do not feel at all upset
When someone offer you a seat!
When you have a wardrobe for all events
And a social life to match it,
And when that garment's old and worn
You do not need to patch it!
When your telephone bill is modest,
Now the fledglings have left the nest,
And when booking a seat in the theatre
You feel you can afford the best,
When your little grandchildren squabble
To climb upon your knee,
Then you can rest assured my friend
That you've reached maturity!

Joan Leahy

Do You Remember?

(Childhood Memories Of 1939-45)

Do you remember
When we were young
Sweets were rationed
Ex-Lax was fun!

Quite a treat -
Raw turnips and 'tater'
Remember your house balancing
On the edge of a crater!

Searching through debris
For old felt hats
Mostly found under stairs -
With their owners, and cats!

Got 6 pence per hat -
A jolly good price -
When I gave you my Guide hat -
And you gave me lice!

Pooling resources -
Front seats at the flicks
Emerging from smoke haze
Necks all in cricks!

Remember too well
Our posh metal fence
- Turned into ammunition
For Civil Defence.

O' happy days
We thought it quite fun
Running to shelter
From bombers and guns!

Norah Page

Years

I have seen, through children's eyes,
So many wondrous sights
That brought to my lips gasps of surprise
To gaze on such delights,
But glasses now clear the way
For advancing years,
Gone is the youth of yesterday
Whose spirit knew no fears.
Imperious youth with uncluttered mind,
Yet care and worries grew,
As youth is simply left behind
And we tread pastures new,
Of the big wide world of adulthood,
Its trials and tribulations
Of paying bills, and being good
To some new-found relations.
Save, as years pass us by
Until policemen look much younger
And then, as at times we cry,
When our lives are torn asunder.
Friends, families, all pass on
Soon it will be my turn
But fears and worries now are gone
As the thoughts of old age I spurn.

G Wright

Age Itself Is Strange

She stands embraced by curling hair,
Loved by all that she would grow to hate,
A newer step to take, no fear of stretching paths,
She sees no need to wait.

The clasping hand unfolds,
From Mother's loving grasp, retreats.
No call goodbye is heard,
Though greeting those she meets.

She climbs the flattened steps,
She'd be pushed down one day,
And pauses at the top,
Looks back, no words to say.

Had thirteen years stacked high,
Her fear would have been real.
And parting of the minds,
Was something she would feel.

She wanders into school
As Mother's hand grows fade
Though she could have softly known
That some hand should have stayed.

And so I see this child,
That inner part of me,
Venturing blindly on,
To pain she can't foresee.

Though I may now do the same,
A cycle without change,
I have the strength to know,
That age itself is strange.

Jillian Shields

Repair The Despair

Oh Lord Jesus, please show us the light
Shield us from the darkness of night
Show us all the good things we've had
Then we'll know life's not so bad.

Those who are lonely - spend hours alone
No physical contact - just a mobile phone
To shake someone's hand or give a cuddle
Or will their mind remain in a muddle?

So Lord Jesus, I don't mean to be rude
Lots can be done with your spiritual food
Release us from the gloom and doom
Bring your light into my darkest room

Give me strength to project your light
To someone else with a similar plight
And raise a smile on numerous faces
Introduce them to the social graces

And those who are at the end of their tether
Renew their faith as we pray together
Dear Lord show them you care
And lighten their world of fear and despair.

Stanley Swann

To Have It All

I gaze through the windows of time seeing past, present and future,
So precious is the moment
I look towards the young, and for a while I feel the enthusiasm,
And I smile
I glimpse at the wisdom of the aged,
And I wonder
I see myself no longer young, and not yet old,
And I sigh

How I loved the wondrous days of my youth
Life was sweet
To be forever young, and forego life's deeper plan
There lies a thought
Could I choose one time above the other?
Not I
But oh that youth and age would merge and fill me
'Full'.

Jean Phillips

Outing On A Summer Day

Every summertime
The village chapel went off for the day
We went by train, left at nine
To Barry Island and the place of Queens
To spend some time by the sea

We were all dressed in our best apparel
Mum in serge coat and best hat like a barrel
I had on best shoes and lovely red dress
We weren't allowed to paddle
In case our knickers got wet

The sea tasted of salt
And made my lips dry
I longed to drink dandelion and malt
However all was great and we're dressed in our best
So we couldn't really prolificate

Long stretched the day
And it was still cool and grey
As always seemed at Barry Island Bay
Then why was it so lovely to be there
Was it the companionship or such happiness rare
Or was it riding the grey rugged mare
Those who dare!

Betsy Williams

My Thoughts On Washdays Past And Present

Then...

Early I must rise this morning
As another washday's dawning.
To get things clean I try to cope
With water hot and bar of soap.
A washing board I use to scrub,
Or dolly legs rotate in tub.

When I have done most of that toil
In copper I put whites to boil,
Then take them out to rinse well through.
(The final rinse with bag of blue).
With mangle then to work I set
And hope it takes out excess wet.

The other items washed today
Are rinsed and mangled the same way.
Then if perchance the day is fine
I peg them on the washing line,
And if to ground they tend to drop
I raise them with a wooden prop.

But if alas the day is wet
No chance to hang them out I get.
So by the fire they have to dry
On clothes horse or a rack up high.
When in a kitchen full of steam
Some new invention is my dream.

Now...

A wonderful machine I've got
That washes, rinses, dries the lot.
Just press a switch and day or night
Electric power makes labour light.
As an invention great it ranks,
To its creator, 'Many thanks'.

Harriet McCaul

Now Will Become Then

For me, now will eventually become then.
Although I still remember then,
Now, as in the present, will eventually become then.
When I'm geriatric and grey,
Then will be remembered as innocence, misunderstood and
active times.
The days of my youth, are still in progress, so I am weaving the future for
then.

Now is schoolwork and exams.
Then was development and mischief.
In comparison to then, now I am mature.
University, work, marriage, children and retirement become
now and then.
Yesterday is then.
Today is now.

Then is antiquity,
Now is modern and development.
Now is each and every moment we are living.
Now is every moment and event we have lived.
Now is a miracle.
Now are the most important days of my life.

Stephen Tuffnell

The Good Old Days

'Congratulations!' said the teacher.
'You've won first prize in English.
You'll be pleased to hear that
The money has gone to the war effort.'
'Delighted!' I thought as she handed me
A scrappy bit of paper.
Where was our teenage fun?
Oh, we found bits here and there,
But boys and girls joined up, went abroad,
Saw things unmentionable, came back
Men and women. Lost, those youthful years.
And yet, and yet, I wouldn't be without it.
Something it's done for me, given me.
Implanted in my heart a deep compassion
For the grieving and the dying, the useless loss,
And I feel sad for the struggles of today.
The worry of drugs, of misuse of body and mind.
In many ways, our lives were easier, uncomplicated
By what we didn't have or know we missed.
But don't give back to me 'the good old days'.
I revel in the present. Now is now, the past
Informs my present, guides my future.
And I rest happy in that promise yet to come.

E Morris

Golden Dreams

Once there was a land,
where the unicorns played,
and fairies were rulers of
all they surveyed.

Giants wandered free as air,
and bluebirds sang without
a care.

I visited this land in golden dreams,
of fairy castles and enchanted streams.

Now I cannot find this land, it faded
away but I remember its beauty to
this very day.

Z Britton

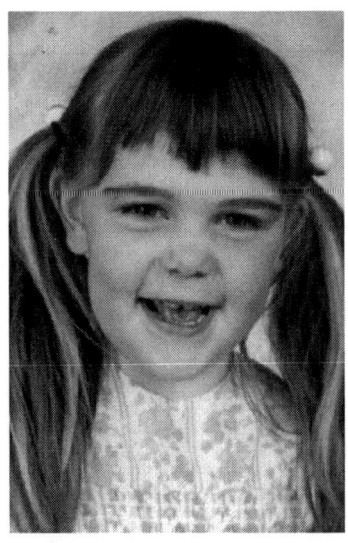

Looking Back . . .

Looking back through the dust of time,
to My far distant childhood days,
I wonder how different it would have been,
had I taken one of the other cross-ways.

I would lie in the meadow, white clouds above,
and daydream of fortune and fame,
to dance to an enraptured audience I longed,
but My chances of that never came.

Fate has not dealt me a very good hand,
still I had laughter and love by the score,
now looking back at old dreams of the past,
I find the yearning is with Me no more.

My youth was filled with excitement and thrills,
new things to experience day by day,
I made many mistakes on the byways of life,
and grew wiser through them on My way.

I'm old now and tired but I've had a good life,
with My wonderful family all around Me,
they'll be My footprints I'll leave in time's sand,
to mark where I've been, don't you see?

Pamela Eckhardt

Now And Then

Now, I am leaving with my boys

And Then, it was just the two of us

Now, I have learnt what life is like

And Then, I learnt from you

Now, I have grown up and seen a different life

And Then, I was young, impressionable and innocent

Now, I am a Woman, a Mother, A Seer

And Then I was a Girl, A Follower, a Doer

Now, I am paving a new life with my boys

And Then, it was just the two of us

Now, My life is different
I am confident
I am independent
I am capable
I am strong
I am now *Me*

And Then, it was *We*

Now, I see freedom

And Then, I saw only a prison

Now I see a light

And Then, I saw only darkness and despair

Now, I am going to be *whole*

And Then, I was broken pieces of a jigsaw

Now, is the end of

And Then ...

Nia Michael

Yesterday's Child

I dammed a stream
And had a dream -
Nothing seemed impossible
I'm yesterday's child

I climbed a tree
And I could see
A wondrous, endless journey
I'm yesterday's child

I lost a friend,
Thought life would end,
But learned that love is lasting
I'm yesterday's child

Now I sit it in my chair
And no one seems aware
Of the wealth I have to share
Because I'm yesterday's child.

Gerallt Wyn Davies

Now And Then . . .

Here I am posing as a seven-year-old with my dear mother
Today I still retain my roguish girlie ways
As the Gaelic expression denotes
She never changed
She is the same three and fourpence
Boy, I ask myself . . .
Are sayings for real?
Then in 1982 I felt very special indeed
I experienced great mental storms
And no woman or man were worthy to rescue me . . .
I now await the Crown of Heaven
For I know this earth is but one big vale of tears
This is a photograph of me aged seven
With my loving mother
Who has always been my faithful protectress
She was my Maud Gonne icon of the swinging sixties
I was indeed a radiant child with my mischievous ways
Now I am worldly-wise
And forging a fruitful destiny into the 21st century
Adoremus te child of Grace . . .

Rita Cleary

In Our Prime

Far away behind the years
Lie our memories half-blind with tears
A life beginning, youth's innocence slowly spent
Mum's clothes horse has made a nice new tent
Hopscotch and marbles
Played with friends who will never die
Skipping and laughing no reason to sit and cry
Rag and bone men came to call
London Liz drove her neighbours up the wall
Making daisy chains in the park
Ringing doorbells for a lark
Picture shows on Saturday, Sunday School the next
Tomato sandwiches for picnics, cycling there and back
Running errands, losing pennies planning to run away
Brownies and Youth Club, playing in the hay
Chips, thrupence a bag, bags of scrumps for free
Mud and tares, grazes on our knee
Cornflakes for breakfast, bread and jam for tea
Swinging on the allotment gates
Picking at the greens left around our plates
Thinking very carefully how to spend 1s.6d a week
Quizzing at the reason why you look before you leap
White mice for pets, chickens in a shed
I had a lot of sisters so I had to share a bed
The roads we used to follow
The trees we used to climb
Don't forget the gentle years
When we were in our prime.

Linda Doel

You're Different Now

Wider concerns were long left behind,
Ambition and envy now play on the mind,
Compassion and justice now meet with derision,
Your status and prestige are based on division.

To question and care no longer in fashion,
Complete competition consuming your passion,
You say it's your age, an inevitable trend,
It's such a shame as you once were my friend.

Jim Riley

But Now It's Christies

It's hard to be told your son has cancer
But worse to find things get better then worse.
I have the uppermost admiration and respect for honesty and I was given that.
But you bury the bad bits, so the shock is that much greater.

We were all spoilt by the dedication of health care workers.
Doctors, nurses, cleaners. They all cared.
Mood swings worse than PMT and pregnancy.
No problem, they were always there.

Fag breaks were the best.
You became a supporter and the supported, each took their turn.
A University degree in the knowledge of coping.
In this tiny spot of concrete, love was really shared.

But now it's time for Christies.

A nurse came 'You've had no food for breakfast or dinner,'
She said. But how can you eat when the stomach cries?
A plate of food kindly wrapped with my name
and reality make you. Strange, pie never tasted so good.

Second day of total body radiation.
The nurses think he's brilliant, he never moved.
Silent and motionless listening to Queen.
Ironic, 'Another One Bites The Dust'.

We've laughed about it since, now he knows the title's meaning.
Still I cannot believe it, radiation.
Something so deadly or life-saving
has no odour, taste or visual sensations, almost not existing. Spooky.

I had never seen anyone so sick.
He allowed me to love him and I knew his threshold had broken.
Oh my God! I had signed for this.
But reality stepped in, there are no choices.

Maria Bernadette Potter

Has The World Gone Mad?

It's a long time before I finally open my eyes. Oh my God! How did I get up here? Was I carried, or did I climb? It doesn't matter now. There's no way back. My exit, that was once so freely called my entrance, stands guarded. Trapped. Trapped with only one way to go. Down! I don't want to go, this isn't my time. It is not fair, why now? I look over my shoulder, there is an obstruction with a pulse still blocking my way to freedom. I get a chill. It's freezing up here, on my own, alone. I'm getting taunted by voices, loud voices. I'm frightened. I wish I were home. There is a noise behind me and this thing grabs my arm, I scream out. I'm at the edge, looking down again. So far down. From this great height, I start to cry. More voices, louder this time, nearer. Scared. I panic. Fright has taken my breath away. Has the world gone mad? But then a soothing voice. A recognisable voice through the madness. Calm in chaos. Saying 'You can make it, Mummy's here, you can make it.' I feel revitalised. I then take a run and leap down the slide. And you know what? I want to do it again!

Jamie Barnes

Middle Years - Mid-Life-Crisis

Once my heart quickened with the spring,
Now I see
Some menace in the weeping willow tree,
Its swelling octopus-embracing arms
I find . . . threatening.
Swishing, sinister thoughts about my mind.
The blushing heather purpling out the bed
Warned me once.
Now creeping, spiky foliage irritates,
Clawing at me as I pause,
Snagging me with its insistence.

In the kitchen, the technicolor world springs
At the window.
The vivid yellow offering of the forsythia
Breasting forth over the sill
Disturbs me 'til,
Blinking, I turn away,
Tired eyes out of tune,
To be affronted by a blast of daffodils,
Trumpeting forth, brassing their 'Gloria'
In silent tribute . . . heralding rebirth.
Acclamation to life-giving tides.
Once my heart quickened with the spring.

Now rhythms all a-cock.
I prick. I do not bleed.
I am nothing.

Yet once my heart quickened with the spring.

Aleene Hatchard

The Butterfly Farm

Emerald green the wings,
Outstretched for flight,
Or nestling nectar
In the noonday sun.
One by one, the entrants pass,
Pause to admire
This 'home-spun' beauty
Bred in the cocooned swathe
Of chapel-breathing Welsh Wales.

Plants grown especially for its needs,
Fed by hands for survival's sake,
Speeds its wingspan.
Brief the breath of freedom
As leaf after leaf holds its heartbeat
In green wonder of soft nurturing.

Emerald green the wings
Outstretched in prayer.
Perfectly pinned on rounded mount
Behind the bright glass in maple frame.
Brazilian beauty, born in exile,
Forever frozen in flight.
Fashionable fancy
Sold from 'The Chapel Font'
Where it is recommended
Visitors may stop and shop.

Janine Vallor

Age Of Innocence

The far-off cry of a child so near
turns your head to the past
for a nameless year.

When all to do was already done
the sounds we remember
the size of the sun.

Build dens in the field we hide from them all
take things from wherever
and trouble would call.

But all of this was just a caper
and money back then
was a creased piece of paper.

The echo is truly the joy and the laughter
still stood in that field
alive ever after.

Lee Severns

Why Does Time Fly?

I can remember being so young,
when time seemed to stand still
and pass by ever so slow.

I couldn't wait for Christmas to come round,
for birthday presents to open and
for my new set of teeth to grow.

The days then seemed so long,
but full of laughter and fun and games
in the local park.

The sun seemed to shine for ever
and we were allowed to play outside
till it was quite dark.

Bike rides, skipping games and picnics,
that took us out exploring woods and fields
often for the whole day.

Rope swings by the brook, hide and seek,
hopscotch in the street,
what enjoyable games we did then play.

Longing to dress up and behave like my two older sisters
and go with them to the dance
at the local hall.

Pictured here, wearing the longed-for shiny patent black leather shoes,
which I thought made me
look so grown-up and tall.

Enjoying my little tartan handbag
like a real lady
full of things I've collected and did treasure.

A clean handkerchief, a comb, a mirror and a purse,
with a few coins in it to buy sweets at the shop,
what a pleasure.

Longing to grow up quickly and properly
and venture out into the big wide world and
see places new.

To meet new people, go on trips
and days out together,
and make friends who'd be reliable and true.

Feeling safe at home, given clothes, toys to play with,
love, affection and care,
yet longing to be independent and mature.

To earn my own money, become a nurse,
a teacher, or a kennel maid,
having my own home and family, and feel so secure.

First, having to cope with lessons at school,
then college, studying hard,
working long hours, how time did drag by.

Wanting to learn to drive, go to the cinema, disco,
for meals and drinks, and to be able
for the first time to fly.

New experiences, becoming slowly older and wiser,
being hurt and upset,
when things sometimes went wrong.

Some relationships failed, leaving you
sad and disillusioned, yet others
became strong.

Now time seems to whizz by, the months,
seasons and years pass by so fast,
and I think, why, oh why?

Didn't I take more time to savour
each passing moment, each experience,
I didn't realise how quickly they would fade and die.

Dot Ridings

Looking Back

How distant now those childhood years,
that once excited a young heart.
Those years of innocence and education,
spent waiting for my life to start.

Out of school and into work,
glad at last to earn a wage.
All that mattered was enjoying life,
youth is such a carefree age.

At twenty-one I fell in love,
an important choice was finally made.
The time had come to settle down,
and watch my freedom slowly fade.

At thirty-one we had three children,
the pride and joy of my life.
Their presence here in this world,
a tribute to my love for my wife.

At forty-six the children were grown.
there had been trouble along the way.
Sometimes the struggle seemed to be too much,
but we chose to fight for a better day.

Looking back now I am forty-eight,
my life I would not attempt to change.
Not for all the riches in this world,
one moment of happiness would I exchange.

For as you grow older in years,
different things seem to matter more.
What treasures cherished by a greedy man,
could replace this family that I adore?

M A Challis

Trainers

'D'you like my new trainers, Gran?'
'Trainers?'
We had 'white rubbers', that's what they were called
The obligatory wear for the long summer hols,
Not that we ever took long holidays as such.
Seventy-one years ago no one took off that much
Our canvas-topped rubbers were pipe cleaned by Mum
Then hung by their laces on the line in the sun
A sign that tomorrow you would be off to Old Leigh,
A train ride. The seaside, the wonderful sea.
The smell of the cockle shells, empty shells mountain high
Brawny men with yoked shoulders half ran along the planks
With dripping baskets of cockles to be boiled in huge tanks.
Past all that to the beach, the beach very small
But as large as all Heaven when you were not very tall.
The tide goes way out leaving miles and miles of soft ooze
Where you wallowed and slid as it sucked at your toes.
Look over your shoulder, your mum is waving away,
Thick china, brown teapot, pound deposits to pay
This is it, it is nearly the end of our day,
'Cup of tea, Gran? You were miles away,'

G Halliwell

September Song

It's time to get the harvest in
We've worked so hard and long
We've had our spring and summer
Now I hear September's song
Spring with all our hopes and dreams
And summer's golden days
Now autumn's mellow fruitfulness
And winter's fickle ways
We have travelled on this train of life
Stopping at every station
Now we have finally arrived
And reached our destination
We now have the cottage of our dreams
With a view to stop the heart
A wonderful family and angel grandchild
With the joy that they impart
We have had our fill of life's surprises
Some good and some bad
We have experienced many happy times
And some have made us sad
It's time to get the harvest in
Now I hear September's song
And with God's blessing we hope
The best is yet to come.

Barbara Anne Smith

You're Older

Fancy having to remind yourself you're
fifty-nine,
all that baggage from the past to leave
with auld lang syne.

The insurers, they hover round like
vultures on their prey,
they push you to sign papers, hardly
let you have your say.

Your family treat you like a wayward
child,
if you tend to disagree they want you
meek and mild.

But, you're a child of Nature and
Nature's running wild,
so, go out like a lion whom no one
has yet beguiled.

Jean Paisley

Times Gone By

When you're tidying out the drawers do you sigh,
When cleaning out the boxes of times gone by?
Bumper annuals or Rupert Bear,
Famous Five up at you stare,
Enid Blyton's animals share the times gone by.

When you uncover infant artwork do you sigh?
The pictures ever vivid of times gone by.
The developing mind has painted,
With imagination untainted,
You're thoughtfully well acquainted with times gone by.

When you're on a nostalgic outing do you sigh
For those longed-for summer days of times gone by.
Making sand pies on the shore,
Often frozen to the core,
Then return to try once more those times gone by.

For the happiness and heartache do you sigh?
Were you right or were you wrong in times gone by?
Did you strive to do your best?
Did you pass the acid test?
Can you with satisfaction rest now time's gone by?

When sitting privately with your thoughts do you sigh
For those ever-changing scenes in times gone by?
Do say thank you for the past
And the memories that last,
Having the privilege of being cast in times gone by.

Walter Crooks

Untitled

I can't believe I looked like this -
Many years ago,
The year was nineteen forty-one -
and war began to show
How different all our lives would be,
Never the same again.
Those of us who were involved, wondered if and when
A day of peace would dawn.

It did! And when it came, we hailed it VE day.
Oh, how we all rejoiced - with parties night and day,
We planned a future in our minds,
Without a future war -
Isn't that, we thought, exactly what peace is for!

Nothing ever goes as planned,
Wars have erupted since.
Dreadful news for all to read - causing all to wince,
When secretly we felt the world may find some harmony
It hasn't yet,
And here I am now, unfit to alter anything
Just another OAP.

Vera Homer

The Key

Let me give you the key
To know yourself and examine
The human liturgy that will nurse
You through your childhood.

Let me give you the key
To unlock the door
That cages you in.

Let me give you the key
That unlocks the universe
And invites you to step in
And take control of a world
Whose engine has been manicured
For greatness.

Robert Vizard

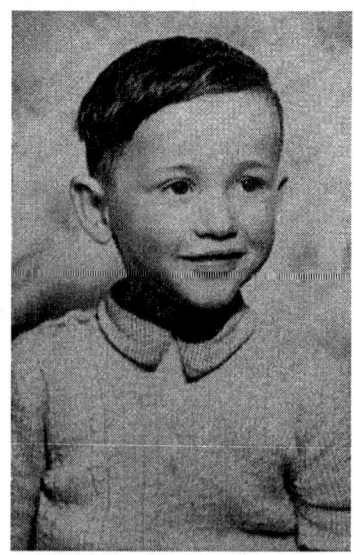

Teenage Girl At Heart

There was once I might have wondered
Why I fail to recognise
This reflection that confronts me
Every morning when I rise
But these days I've ceased to worry
If the mirror's telling lies
In that unfamiliar image
With the wrinkled stranger's eyes

I refuse to follow fashion
Or to suffer for my art
For my dreams are still out dancing
While my body falls apart
Just because I'm growing older
Why should that mean I must start
Feeling grown up when I'm happy
As a teenage girl at heart?

David Gasking

O For The Wings

When I was four I wanted to be an angel in the Nativity
like my friend. I made myself a pair of wings. For a week
I wore them to the shops and to the park and cried each night
when my mother made me take them off for bed.

When I was fourteen I hated my mum and dad.
I *knew* I was a changeling and dreamt of hidden papers
that proved my lineage to someone famous, or sudden accidents
that led to my adoption by my favourite teacher.

When I was twenty-four I envied all my friends who were
stepping out nightly or walking up the aisle. I didn't have a man
and blamed my ginger hair and glasses. I wanted to be this
or that or *anything* that wasn't how I saw myself.

When I was thirty-four I was mired in the mud of motherhood
and duty while all my friends were walking out on theirs.
I hovered on the threshold jealous of their certainty,
but I knew I'd never make that change of address.

When I was forty-four I was stuck in a dead-end job
at a desk that was also going nowhere. I looked back on my life
and wept for all the opportunities and turnings missed
that (I knew for *certain*) would have changed my life.

Now I am fifty-four I've passed safely through my Change.
Wiser now, I count the blessings of my marriage, home
and family. Finally content with who I am, I look forward
to seeing what my remaining decades bring.

When I'm eighty-four I will tell my great grandchildren
'My dears, I've had a good life, I wouldn't change a thing.'
But when I reach the pearly gates, I hope St Peter pats me kindly
on the head and says '*This* time you can keep the wings.'

Carolyn Garwes

To Age

Now I am getting old and grey
My youthful zest is lost;
My inhibitions thrown away,
No longer do I count the cost.

Time passes at a whirlwind pace,
Tomorrows seem to melt away.
Each morning woken by God's grace
To new horizons day by day.

Spring's blossom breaks the buds of May;
The busy drones awake the wayside flower;
The bluebells sound a clarion call,
The diving swallows build their nests.

The thunder's roll, the lightning's flash,
Soft rain falling on my cheek;
The ocean's roar, the wavelet's splash,
The lazy stream, the snow-capped peak.

Age is a time for reflection,
When the intellect is stirred,
Seeking a lost perfection,
In every deed and word.

The river of contentment is found
In simple pleasure with a friend;
Song of a bird, a magic sound,
The sunset's glow when clouds descend.

Noelle Hill

My Grandfather Says . . .

Sun splinters through tall windows,
Scattering over wooden desks,
Neatly stacked in rows.
Chalk dust,
Hangs heavy,
Mingling the smell of mouldy old texts.
Discipline rules.
Stern masters stand erect,
Canes standing tall.
Silence reigns.
Neat pupils,
Ready to learn,
Recite their lessons perfectly,
No mistake tolerated,
All homework done.
The masters feared, yet respected for their learning.

Not like today,
No canes,
The harshest punishment expulsion,
More oft than not detention or suspension.
Does little good,
To kids these days - a joke.
No silence reigns,
The teachers aren't respected,
For the knowledge they possess,
But hated and scorned for their learnings.
No neat pupils,
Little homework done.
Nothing my grandfather ever would have dared.

In his day,
He says,
Respect and discipline were expected,
Work was done,
And neatness demanded.
All but gone in this day and age, he grumbles.

In all but a few.
A few who still toil.

Not like my grandfather's day,
How things have changed,
How he has watched,
What he has seen, this he tells now to me.

Tell me now quickly,
We're really not that bad,
Yes things have changed,
But not all for the worst.

Elaine Wilkin

My Family

When I was born in forty-one
I had one sister and one brother.
A two-bedroomed house that stood in a field
A strict father and a loving mother.
As the years went by our family grew
Until there were six of each.
Not a happier family would anyone find
And that's not a figure of speech.
We were all happy as time went by,
We went out to school each day,
With orders from Mum to hurry up home,
Not time to go out to play.
We all had our duties that we had to do
From potato picking to washing the dishes
The times were hard but even so
Mum and Dad tried to fulfil all our wishes.
On Christmas Eve, armed with our sacks,
We'd climb up the stairs to our beds.
A doll or a tractor we'd hope to find
Nuts and games and books to be read.
Now we're grown and gone our own ways
With families of our own
I often sit down and think of those days
And say to myself how the time has flown.
Our mum and dad are now at rest
One of our brothers as well,
But I wouldn't change one of them,
There are too many tales to tell.
We're there for each other all of the time
Wherever, whatever, whenever.

J E Nicholls

Growing Old

When I was young I used to laugh at Grandma's funny ways,
Today I am a grandma and recall those far-off days
To my grandchildren I seem very strange -
they often laugh at me
The things I do - the things I say -
are laughed at frequently
I scoff at convention -
I've no intention
of following the latest trends
They laugh at my hats and unusual garb,
but that doesn't bother me
Being old and 'comfortable',
my life suits me perfectly.
If I wear something over ten years old,
they say 'That is back in vogue!'
'So what?' I say, as I walk on
wearing ancient brogues.
I'm at an age where I please myself,
I'm in my second flush,
Like a teenager I don't give a hoot -
I am in no rush.
If I wear scarlet with polka dots
and a feather boa round my neck
I have the nerve to wear it now
although I'd look a wreck.
Old age can be pleasant
If you put things in perspective
I have my ills and take my pills -
Alas, *not* contraceptive!
Those days have gone, I'll carry on
Enjoying every minute -
Appreciate my blessings,
my life and people in it.

Myrtle Wright

Whatever Will Be Will Be

Years ago when I was young
There were so many things that had to be done.
I wanted to sing, I wanted to dance
I wanted to go and paint in France.
All these things I could have done
Life was before me, excitement and fun.
Then I let it all slip away
Because on a cold winter's day
I met a man at a local dance.
Of course I did not want to go to France,
I did not want to sing and dance.
All I wanted was to be at his side,
All I wanted was to be his bride.
It all seemed so simple then, we did not stop to think,
The future looked so rosy but it all went by in a wink.
What became of all our dreams?
What became of all our plans?
What became of all our schemes?
It was all taken out of our hands.

Now it is too late, or was it just fate
That made us what we are, or was there a special star
To follow, a certain plan, written out by a special man?
Our pathway is chosen, we know it has to be.
As we grow older, of course we can see.
Whatever will be will be.

Christina M Sturman

Flashes Of My Past

In idle pose I languish with thoughts of years gone by
As sun gives way to twinkling stars in velvet studded sky
Within the circles of my mind relive my childhood dreams
How vividly I can recall my many youthful schemes.

I often stray through memory's lane to when I was 'knee-high'
Each day a new adventure, and I often wonder why
Cocooned within my mother's arms, could this not always be?
The comfort of her tender love, its warmth surrounding me.

My teenage years, a wondrous time, life's lessons to live through
For was it really me out there who found so much to do!
When life was as a whirlwind, each adventure brought a laugh
And then one day, out of the blue I met my 'other half'.

But now the bloom of youth has passed, and many friends have gone
Not there to fill that empty space, not there to call upon
Often dulled with aching pain on rising from my bed
But young at heart and strong of mind and clear within my head.

Fleeting glances of a past that cannot be again
Just my imaginations within my heart remain
For age, in its advancing years has brought me peace of mind
To taste afresh the fount of life of a true and simple kind.

To live each day and please oneself with a spirit that is free
No pressing airs and graces - to be just simply me
Surrounded by a loving brood seems life is not too bad
To see in them the zest of youth I know that I once had.

Barbara Davies

As Time Passes By

As the sun rises at the dawn of a new day once again
And the grandfather clock signals another hour gone
We know it's another day ended and another day started
For the door to yesterday's youth has now closed and
today opens a new one.

As the first of many milestones in my life approaches
The worries have changed and attention has to be paid.
For once I worried if the sun-kissed daisies would make a chain
But now decisions to sculpt my life have to be made.

The anticipation of ripping open crisp, fresh gifts, just out of reach
And the beat of our hearts skipped when we saw our first crush
look our way.
The longing we felt to be the greatest person we could, to fulfil
our dreams
All the feelings which can't be re-created
But we try to every day.

When we were young we were constantly in awe of older children
But now we are the ones setting an example to the carefree
souls of today
And along with joy comes responsibility to be accepted
Although we dodge them, they build with added stress in every way.

The once carefree days of innocent youth have slowly disappeared
And have been replaced with the attitude-tainted maturity
Of the grown child ready to face the big wide world
And build on the experiences that came together to create
her personality.

Hollie Cheadle (15)

The Farm Boy

(Dedicated with fond memories to Agnes Munn)

Five decades ago a farm boy was I
A long steep Scotch hill on my bike I would fly
To West Auchincarroch Farm owned by John Munn
After school and at weekends for milking and fun

Seasonal work it was regular fun
When men cut the corn then the hare he would run
The boys would chase after the hare in the corn
When daylight had gone we would sleep till next morn

Each autumn the tatties would spring forth anew
At howking the tatties I joined the long queue
Long earthy drills of spuds of the best
We picked as the autumn leaves fluttered to rest

Brown Ayrshire and black and white Friesian cows
Were milked twice a day some help I allowed
I mucked out their stalls and fed them some hay
Then biked my way home at the end of the day

On quiet autumn days when the work it slowed down
The farmer's wife Agnes Munn called us around
For strawberries and cream from a tall earthen jug
With fried savoury dough how your tastebuds would chug

My pay was five florins on Saturday night
At the end of the week it was such a delight
Agnes Munn in her land rover drove me back home
To that farm of my childhood in dreams I still roam

Roy A Millar

An Old Battered Wooden Box

An old battered wooden box with treasures so rare
A photograph of you as a young girl
Smiling, sticking out your tongue,
Enjoying your holiday without a care.

Love letters faded, carefully tied
To your Tom with news from the hospital
Of how your precious babe had died,
You declared your love for ever,
And said you would leave him never.

A piano recital programme well folded recalling that day
All dressed in my new finery I sat down to play
You and Dad in the front row clapping madly
I proceeded to strike the keys so very badly.

Drawings and letters from grandchildren small
Depicting you so tiny and Dad so tall,
Tales ranging from football and two o'clock fishing
Adventures large or small, none were missing.

A newspaper cutting so aged and small
Announcing the death of your darling Tom
You were so brave as I recall
The end of a remarkable love story had come,
You carried on with your daily tasks
But love never dies, it always lasts.

A new final item, clean and white
Is added to your collection,
It does not tell the tale of your brave fight
And how you soldiered both day and night.
Now in Tom's arms you peacefully sleep
Your old, battered wooden box I will keep.

Linda Lawton

It Was All On A Summer's Day

It was all on a summer's day when the
meadows looked fresh and green after
a shower of rain,
I walked upon a carpet of soft green grass
that was peppered with wild flowers of
almost every species native to our shores

I pondered for a while and thought of peace
in the world, and being there in the meadow
it seemed as if there were no problems in
the world.

I could have stayed there for the rest of my
days. Passing through the meadow I came
upon a waterfall which in itself was
magnificent. But looking deeper it made
me think of all the anger in the world. Its
force and power were so tremendous,
Fearlessly unstoppable.

Life is so like a waterfall, being born as a
trickle of water, then dying in a tremendous
power surge.

It is such a strange world we all live in.

Francis Joseph Lawton

Whisper In The Wind

As the wind blows it carries to me,
The smell of the pine, echoes from the trees.
Faint whispers that are carried in the air,
Voices from the past, but nobody's there.

Childhood memories of places I have been,
Now left far behind, they seem but a dream,
Pictures and images stored in the back of my mind,
Released to tell a story of a life left behind.

Memories of childhood playing in the sun,
The air was filled with laughter,
Life was so much fun,
Now we're older and wiser too,
But the children are still playing as we used to do.

Schooldays were the best days of our lives
We learned to work, to play, we were so alive.
When we left, some moved away,
Losing contact with friends, we saw every day.

As the wind blows it carries to me
Memories of what life used to be,
Voices from the past, that are no longer there
But the memories are just a whisper in the air.

Andrew Brian Zipfell

The Good Old Days

It seems another lifetime my youth - my life
When outside toilets were visited
With newspaper, and candles for light

Damp bedrooms, hot water bottles, airing your clothes
Press on the mirror - where steam arose
Out of jumpers - hand-knitted of course
And just when you thought things couldn't get worse

The rent man would call - no money to spare
Quick, everyone hide under the stairs
Keep quiet, don't move, wait 'til he's gone
Maybe next week we can give him some.

Values were different - no need to lock doors
Everything I have - everything yours
Not that you'd want it - tin baths and the like
Makes you appreciate the small things in life

My mom would wash and in the yard
We had a mangle - to turn it was hard
My sons of today would have a fit
To think their D&G, Gucci and Versace were put through it

Maybe not all good, but not half bad and in many ways
Some would say 'The good old days'

Gloria Summerfield

The Gardener's Boy

Aged six, I made a friend (he seemed
a god!) three times my years.
My father's Homburg I esteemed,
but Wol it was of whom I dreamed,
whose absence prompted tears.

Digging, mowing lawns in strips,
or chopping in the shed,
he'd tell me all his country tips,
and make me firewood battleships;
we'd share his cheese and bread.

Bonfire days, redbreast attending,
spuds in cinders sang.
Shirtless summer sport expending
puny fists his strong arms fending -
Life with laughter rang.

Then came the war. Wol went to sea;
to boarding school went I.
He sent a pencil-sketch to me:
his ship from bombers fighting free.
(I binned it, on the sly.)

Years later, when we met again,
it wasn't as before.
He seemed less tall than other men;
my accent had been poshed by then:
scar-faced, he called me 'Sir'!

Bernard Brown

A Long Time Ago

When the long summer day was totally spent
We were safe to sleep in our ridge tent

A straw pillow to rest our head
A stitched over blanket and that was our bed

Up in the morning, bright and gay
To decide what to do the rest of the day

Hopscotch, skipping, a ride on your bike
Or better still - play by the brook

Splash in the water and pretend to be fishing
With a cane, length of string and a pin for the hook

A tub of ice cream or a soda pop
Could be bought for three pence from the corner shop (old tuck shop)

Days seemed long and kids were safe to be outside as late as they could
Playing games or going for a walk in the wood

Enjoying life the way kids should

D E Bundy

The Unseen

I do not enclose a photograph
as I destroyed every one.
My sister holds a snapshot
that's of me at twenty-one.
But I'm afraid I look the same
and don't want to be known.
I crave no recognition
when I'm walking round the town.
My past is gone, I need no proof
of how I looked in far gone days.
I do not live in memories,
for me my life runs new each day.
I do not seek attention
I live here on my own,
I do my best for others,
my face I want not known.
Those early days are best forgot,
in misery I do not dwell.
I've lived my life, achieved a lot
and have no tales of woe to tell.
I so respect my privacy,
I just look forward to each day
and then at dusk I stop, to kneel
and thank the Lord, to Him I pray,
'Dear Lord I thank You for the pleasure
of giving me a day to treasure.
Perhaps the chance to give a hand,
I bless You for this life and land.'
I thank you all at Triumph House,
it's nice to see my words typefaced,
You know me by those words and letters,
but none will ever know my face.

Channon Cornwallis

Then And Now

When I was young
I felt the world
Was young with me
And bright,
Songs and laughter
Filled my ears
I had no thought
Of tired old age
My God was good
And I would stay
Forever in the month of May!

But time was stealing
Youth away;
At last I realised one day
That spring and summer now had gone
I woke to find one misty dawn
That autumn had its story!
For in these calmer,
Slower days,
I now had time to give God praise
And share with Him these golden days
And give to Him the glory!

Pearl Reynolds

Untitled

When I was a kid
We would skip
Play top and whip
Hopscotch and Postman's Knock
No drugs, no thugs, no money
Them days have gone
Life goes on

H Ratcliff

Lost And Found

Now almost halfway through the fourth decade of my life,
I pause to reflect on the changes that have occurred . . .
As a naive youngster, when asked my age, I immediately replied
four and a half, emphasising the half!
Unexplainable impatience watching the year drip-feed slowly by,
Waiting for the long, warm summer holidays and the numerous
presents at my birthday and Christmas-time.
By comparison, time is now whizzing by and many is the time that
I have wished to halt its unstoppable march to give me those vital,
extra, few, precious hours.
This leads me to thoughts of friends at my different schools, now
scattered globally,
To others, who sadly have now left this mortal coil.
At my recent class of 1979 school reunion, I went with visions of
youthful, acne-scarred, nascent adults as I remembered them when we left
in 1986,
Lo and behold, fifteen years later, I had trouble identifying a lot of them
as good living and unforgiving time had ravaged their physical
appearances.
University, and undoubtedly, the happiest phase of my life
I remember attending lectures and practicals during the day and
dancing the night away with no ill effects the next day!
Yet now, gout rakes and strains my joints making this an impossibility!
Marriage and fatherhood and the contentment, happiness and anchoring
stability this has brought to an otherwise Bohemian lifestyle.
My prospering career in which I go from strength to strength.
As I see my reflection in the daily ablutions and morning ritual of shaving, my
face which appears to be unchanged like the picture of Dorian Gray.
However, the photograph album is testament to this lie!
Physically, mentally and spiritually, I have gained and lost in the
wonderful encyclopedia that is life!

Robin Halder

Home Fire Reflections

Like a magnet, it drew us to itself,
this warm-hearted, glowing friend.
The trivial round found cheering respite there.
Evenings, it brought us to unity;
and we talked about our day,
the stresses melting perceptibly.
As hearts responded, reluctant tongues relented,
rapport dissolving reserve:
those flickering fingers chased shadows, not
merely from the walls, but from the spirit,
and chatter sparkled with laughter.
Late evenings, soft music from the wireless
was the quieting close to our busy day.

But, then, a bright glare displaced the glow:
a noisy icon, often divisive.
Television had arrived.

Now, as the world's misery pours from its screen,
an enduring image lightens black tedium:
it is of father, armchair ensconced, reading.
At peace by a glowing fire.

Ron Hails

A Teenager In The Fifties

This photograph is one of my favourites
As it shows me at the age of eighteen
Posing out there on the rooftops
Nearly fifty years have gone by in between.
We had climbed out of our bedroom window
Up in the attic of our residential college
It was an all-female institution
A centre of excellence and knowledge.
We often climbed out there to have picnics
Or make plans looking up at the sky
We had no worries, no doubts or no fears.
Though we were sitting out four storeys high.
I was wearing my gym uniform
As we had PE nearly every day,
We were training to be primary teachers
Students no longer 'live in' today.
This was our most daring pastime
We'd have been punished but we never got caught
There were so many rigid rules and regulations
'Twas by very strict nuns we were taught.
We were teenagers then, in the Fifties,
And were still expected to do as we were told,
Girls were expelled for quite simple misdemeanours
So we felt quite rebellious and bold.
Perhaps we were really too innocent
Compared to teenagers of today,
But I personally feel young folk grow up too soon
They can't wait to leave home and get away
Still whenever I look at this photo, I only remember
All the fun and good times that we had.

Mary Anne Scott

Why?

As I walk down the street
I begin to feel the heat
People stopping and staring
Shouting at me without caring.
But I have done nothing to them
I was born with this face
That they find so disgraced
They point at me
They taunt me
They even go so far as to haunt me
As I walk around the block
I see kids playing hopscotch
I wish I could smile just like them
But when they see me they just run
I'm so sorry to spoil all their fun
But I have done nothing to them
As I nearer my front gate
My legs and body no more shake
I begin to feel safe again
As I put my key in the door
I hear them shout another name at me, once more
I shout back, 'Please, no more'
As I crouch down now
On the other side of the door.
Will it be like this forever
Always looked at as strange
One thing's for sure
To come out of all this
Is that I'll never give into their games.

Terence Johnson

Betrayal

It was in the market place
I heard news of you today.
Though summer is almost here
I will not feel its blessed warmth
For hope that was inside my heart
Vanished instantly for me.
This year my heart will not let me see
The daffodils that sway, and dance,
Upon the hillside.
There melody, is not for me
It will rain and the sun will shine
But inside my cloak of grief
I will only feel the pain
Of loss of you.
Yet! Not wanting to! My heart still stands
A beggar at your door
I have to tell myself 'no more!' 'No more!'
And set myself free, from loving you
And you not loving me!
From this day on I have no claim to thee.
My news was, that you married last spring,
And gave someone else a wedding ring!

D Brook

Now And Then

I think of things all of the while
  And not just now and then
Cry for the suffering of Animals
  At the brutal hands of men
I am with them in their suffering
  Am tormented by their pain
And not just now and then
  But again and again and again
I wonder at humanity
  At the sadism in its blood
It leans so easily to evil
  And so reluctantly to good
And yet it sings its praises
  As though man is king and queen
Superior to everything
  But man is cruel and mean
Monarchs over one and all
  And in their ignorance they say
'We are superior on this Planet'
  Yet killing everything in their way
Now and then is not enough
  Dark cultures must be fought
Every second of every day
  Civilised ways they must be taught
For humanity is rampant
  Trampling on each other
And our precious little Animals
  When we should all be Dad and Mother
Loving all that is around us
  No matter where or when
Every second of every day
  And not just now and then

Thus on my journey through my life
   I learn and wonder when
Concern will happen all the time
   And not just now and then

Clare Marshall

Dancing Was Our Cure

We worked hard in the job we loved, gave all we had
My did we feel good.
We had some dear bosses, who were not too happy
And at times they gave us hell, we worked out why
They were so and we felt a little sorry for them as they were
Now getting on a bit, we knew we were young.
Nothing that a hot soak didn't put right, on the handmade designer
Dress and to the hop we go, returning like Cinderella
One of the most handsome who one could take anywhere.
Had a strict home, even the army back then was milder
When he packed to be dancing partner, fibbed a little a regimental do.
A life has passed between then and now, the dancing ceased
A family reared and loved ones lost.
An invitation to the hop to help an old girl's ache, first to call,
The handsome bachelor dancing partner from away back then.

Margaret Gleeson Spanos

Longevity

I'm a 'has been'
In wheelchair.
Memories sweet
Relatives none, to share.

Memories treasured
In mind to last
Sorrow ever
Love true, now past.

I dream away
How long? Not sure
Dreams all fade
Memories mine, endure.

Friends come, go
Time slowly passes
Loneliness ever grows
When I mislay my glasses.

Life must go on
I know full well
My vigorous health gone
I'm grateful for their help.

Earth's blessings divine
Mankind's gifts many
For span of life
Thanks give for longevity.

Ivy Lott

Viewpoint

The extended telescope of time reveals
my life's progression between the womb and tomb.
Looking back, the telescope reversed, I see
the distant vistas of my past
with the clarity of pure water in a glass.

Using the magnified perspective to look into the future
I foresee time collapsing inwards on itself,
rushing to engulf me like a tidal sea.

Then, what use am I, what have I been, what may I become
before I eventually succumb? I cannot twist the rope of sand
as the hour-glass measures out my time,
nor lure it back to cancel one word of it, one line.

But I can open the citadel in which my memories are stored;
come, ransack the treasures locked away beneath the vaulted arch,
inquire within, the castle is open, entrance free on any day.

Those who trust in others must never be betrayed
whose lives are still before them, to whom debts should be repaid.
My mind's compressed experience and complimentary skills
are free for those who wish to dip within my deepest wells.

It really is time to give back what has been given me,
to care for growing children and those who now stand tall.
To share in their unclouded views and join with Heaven above
in offering them the supreme gift, the blessed gift of love.

And in return it may transpire
that fairest fortune grants to me
part of a heart, a heart that is true,
to hold in memory's store;
just a part, a small part of you,
and I'm yours for evermore,
yours for evermore.

Norman Meadows

The Way We Were Then

We cannot stop or delay time -
Stop a bus, or taxi, but *not* time.
Things have changed over the years -
We could always leave open our back door -
And all the cousins slept happily on the floor -
But times were hard before World War II -
Low wages, and no modern conveniences -
Dinner was perhaps sheep's head broth -
Only Christmas lunch was a treat!
Father would bring in the chicken and pluck it
Its head inside a dolly tub the poor little fowl
Feathers flew all over, this made Granny growl!
No chicken barbecues then or Chinese Take-aways!
Mother slaved over a hot stove in those days.

I remember a week we couldn't wait until Friday -
Time dragged on until our wage payment
All our thoughts were on the dance on Saturday
And months crawled slowly until our annual holiday.
Years went by and technology advanced -
Televisions and computers came and holidays abroad
Time was altering what we knew then -
But now - we hear of floods, rail disasters, melting icebergs!
And so recently the countryside is in complete chaos!
Our cattle thrown on a burning pyre -
Surely this was not God's desire!
Is He punishing us for the state of the nation?
What then we knew as the present is now the past
And the future is now the present!
But, I knew those days and have seen the change -
But will still think of them as 'the good old days'.

M E Smith

Will Christmas Never Come

At the age of six
I thought it would never come.
Twenty-four more days to go.
Around the house, hidden from sight
Were parcels for you not to see.
Till you accidentally found
At the top of the wardrobe
Much too high, a doll
With golden hair,
But much too high to get back down,
The chair began to slip,
The wardrobe, with you
Inside, onto the bed fell.
Trapped like a criminal
You had to stay,
The doll is not for you.
But now, there's no
Time to hide parcels
Anywhere for twenty
Years later, it's a last
Minute rush to the shops
On Christmas eve.
Then comes the delight
Paper sparkling bright, and late that night,
Round the tree they go.
Why has time grown so short,
Is the world moving faster, or what?

Audrey Allen

Reflections

Reach back to a time in memories past
When life was so simple and plain
When cars and planes were rare to see
And few people lived for gain

When street games were the done thing
Hide and seek and kick the can
Top and whip and even hopscotch
And tick the others, as they ran

Ice cream came in only one way
By a cart pulled along by a horse
Lollipops were frozen in the shops
And cost just a penny and no more

When the cinema was called the picture house
And all films were in black and white
The most violence that was ever shown
Was the cowboy and Indian fights

Summers came and we never saw rain
It seemed that the sun shone each day
Every hour was the length of a week
And there was nothing to do but play

My heart is so sad for children today
When our freedom they will never know
The innocence of a time gone by
Kept in memories that will never let go.

Gillian Mullett

The Years Between

Over long years I've read many excellent books in bed.
William Shakespeare, Brothers Grim, Wordsworth, Dickens and Kipling,
But now I'm getting old I find that Catherine Cookson comes to mind,
And other authors of her kind.

Silent pictures with Chaplin - the clown of them all,
And Shirley Temple, who made our tears sometimes fall.
Now, it's Tom Cruise who makes our hearts beat faster,
With 'real-life' films of love and disaster.

Young kids swept chimneys and worked down the pits,
Now it's school, college and 'uni' and how to keep fit.
As a child 'Magic Lanterns' were really a treat,
Now it's tele or internet when I put up my feet.

Man once walked upon the moon - now we will visit there quite soon.
I saw the Zeppelin when I was three, but Concorde I've yet to see.
British beef was good for me,
Now it's GM foods and BSE.

Prim BBC quizzes where there for us for free,
But now we pay out on the lottery.
Graham Bell's telephones were a real breakthrough,
Now it's mobile phones, direct to you.

The computer sitting in my spare room
Could fly a spaceship to the moon.
Abacus, fingers and our thumbs
Are now redundant for doing our sums.

Many things have changed it's true, but war and greed never do.
From the Vikings to Kosova, wars are still the same.
It's simply *people* who are to blame.
But with strong will and incentive we would all find
The world could have peace for all mankind.

Milly Hatcher

Changing Scenes - Now And Then

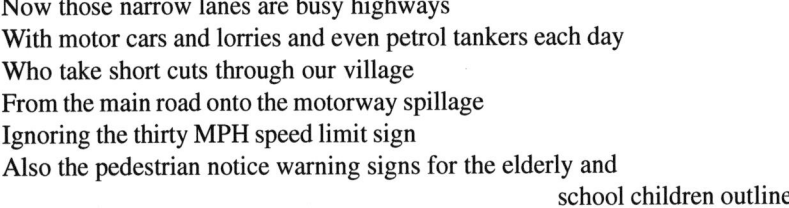

The little village where I was born
Has grown up over the years so forlorn
From the twentieth century into the twenty-first
With changing scenes some good, some much worse
So tranquil in my childhood and school days
When the lanes were a pleasure to walk or cycle along the byways
To school or to the village shop
Which only seems like yesterday but alas it's not.

Now those narrow lanes are busy highways
With motor cars and lorries and even petrol tankers each day
Who take short cuts through our village
From the main road onto the motorway spillage
Ignoring the thirty MPH speed limit sign
Also the pedestrian notice warning signs for the elderly and
                                    school children outline
The road safety measures which are just a few
Of modern times we now have to adhere to.

The fields and farmland where we once played as kids
Have now disappeared to make way for building project bids
The farm buildings converted into housing estates
And the country cottages modernised to date
Instead of the old coal fire and cooking range
We now have gas and electricity facilities, another change
With water cisterns on the spot
Not the old garden pump and wash tub trough

Time waits for no one as life's journey changes each day
From the early age until maturity we accept along the way
Now the lifestyle of today seems to give us more time and leisure
But the old ways I think gave us more pleasure
In a world of contentment each day doing our best
Now unfortunately life's experiences in a world of unrest are
                                    so selfish and hard to digest.

Nancy Owen

Memories

As a child I roamed the countryside,
Taking sandwiches and lemonade to drink,
With my sister, hills we climbed
Leaving many miles behind,
Starting out early morning and returning in time for bed.
Enjoying every mile of grassy slope or wooded hill,
Running streams and sunny banks,
With never enough time to play,
No fears or worries of modern day,
A child today I can relate,
The anger of not going further than the garden gate,
The boredom and the fear,
No freedom as of yesteryear.

V Harding

Introspection

We comment on the world's ways, are trite and superficial -
Speak empty words and often frown and try to sound judicial.
But like a shiny mirror, that reflects life's ongoing show,
We polish up our surface but we rarely look below.

Reflect, how often we condemn the acts of fellow men,
And how often do we, truthfully, compare ourselves to them.
Our greatest sin is self delusion, and our false pride has lit,
The only dismal, smouldering, fire that warms the hypocrite.

Sometimes we are forced to look - *we too are criticised*,
But our self indulgent focus, transforms our faults and fears of failing,
To confidence restored again and egos safely sailing
Upon the shallow waters of our self esteem,
Ignoring the opportunity there might have been
To have looked and really seen below the surface of the stream.

But if we did the sharp recoil of unaccustomed touch,
Like cold fingers on our inmost selves would not accomplish much.
For we must look and look again and learn to bear the pain;
To live life with a false perspective surely is to live in vain.
We must strive to be complete, face what we are anew,
Let our delusions die and to ourselves be true.

Derek Meredith

From Counting Time To Making Time Count

Faces etched in glowing coals.
Empty, lost, staring souls!
Prodding poker to make them red.
Glowing in their cosy bed!

Frolicking in bluebell woods.
A sea of swaying aqua hoods.
Seeking fairies in mossy dell.
Toadstools have their tales to tell.

Eyes glued to the clock; an endless beat.
Waiting for a special treat!
Uncontrolled craving to be free.
Every minute eternity!

Beetroot face meets a stranger's grin.
Embarrassment seeps from within!
Pythagoras and complex French verb.
Passions that are hard to curb!

Young shoulders can't carry an old head.
Wisdom must be learnt, instead!
Grey hairs may master that raging fire,
With understanding of desire!

Young ones grow at amazing pace.
Soon seek their own resting place!
Autumn's years teach us to count our days.
Helping others in many ways!

Eyes are glued to the clock no more.
Life's boredoms have found a cure!
We've obtained the key to living.
Happiness only comes from giving!

Val Spall

40 Year Span

At 20 I thought I knew it all
The world was an oyster at my feet
But I was shy and retiring then
Still unsure of life and its mysteries

In my thirties, married with family of three
Life very hectic, little time for pleasantries
A constant round of bottles and nappies
Oh for a good night's sleep

On reaching 40 I thought, I'm old, oh dear
My life is nearly over, I fear
Children still dependant, life still very busy
But as if to compensate for getting older
I acquired a little more wisdom and experience
And became a little bolder

By 50 I thought, well, this is it
I'm over the hill, so be it
Universities, weddings, oh the finance
Sacrifices made to give them all a chance

Now just past 60, I'm looking back
Where have all those years gone
So caught up in family affairs
You feel life has just passed you by
Answering their questions, allaying their fears
Tending to their problems, drying their tears

I'm a very proud mum of my three children
And now a grandmother of four
I'm glad I made time to spend with them
For time is the most precious gift
That you can give your children

Phyllis L Stark

Doppelgangers

Once I was
The only Rupert, the only one
Or seemingly
Of course there had always
Been famous ones,
Prince Rupert and Rupert
Brooke
But they were distant
In time
As I got older other Ruperts
Appeared
What once had been a trickle
Became a tide
Ruperts sprang up from far
And wide
From being almost alone
I had
Developed a clone
Whose
Name was Rupert Smith
And who
Reviewed last night's
TV
For the Guardian.

Rupert Smith

Now And Then

Now and then I'll have you know,
I've had the urge to have a go,
At something that I've had in mind,
For some time past, and then I find,
I'm thinking that I'll do it later
Because just now I cannot cater.

For all the things it will involve,
The problems I will have to solve.
Most of all, though it's not funny,
I fear I do not have the money
I know I can't indulge myself,
So the idea goes upon the shelf.

But that was then and this is now,
You've managed very well somehow.
With a good wife and children, you have been blessed,
Of happiness you've had the best.
Grandchildren too have come along,
To add to your life's sweetest song.

You've had your ups and downs, it's true,
But if you take the long term view,
There's nothing much that you would change,
Be assured that is not strange.
For some there is that silly vow,
'If I'd known then what I know now'.
Don't think that way, just understand,
For each of us our life is planned.

Frank William Beever

Southport 1957

Just occasionally,
We would ignore the beckoning bus stop,
My mother and I,
Probably owing to much juvenile imploring,
And head over the bridge to the cinder track

To Hesketh Park Station with its coal-yard siding,
Traditional dim booking hall and waiting room,
(A small fire burning in the grate in winter).
Double thump of the ticket machine signalling each purchase,
We would emerge into platform daylight,
Glancing up and down shimmering rails,
In habitual expectation.

Half a mile to Meols Cop in a familiar bottle-green
Electric unit, along a well-known track
Tracing back under the road bridge,
Glimpsing the footbridge and signal box,
Near which I so often stood to watch,
Notebook in hand; past the engineering works,
Where rolling stock, often from distant Morecambe and Heysham,
Waited for repair.

Then unchartered territory - places I couldn't place -
The line to St Luke's, back-yards and railway cuttings,
Railed off and overgrown,
Like so many others if only I'd known,
Before the last short crawl into the town.

Fifteen minutes of transport with boyish delight,
A brief mile or so to fuel a young appetite
For places, brochures, timetables and travel -
A lifetime's journeying beginning to unravel.

Jonathan Stocker

Youthful Dreams

I really used to love Meccano -
My great aim - to own a Number Ten;
But we were rather poor
And though I asked them often and again
A Number Nine was all I could aspire to.

When I retired I bought a Number Ten
But that first fine dream of youth departed
And hardly had I started
But the eyes grew dimmer
And the withered hands started to shake!
I don't think I'll ever make
That wonderful crane
That appeared in all the manuals -
It's just a tortured phantom from the past
Like those Billy Bunter books
And the Greyfriars' Holiday Annuals!

Leo Taylor

Newmarket In The 20s and 30s

The fair was held on Tanners field,
Top if Icewell Hill.
The circus on the Severals,
Oh what a thrill.
Sunday was for Sunday school,
Morning and afternoon.

Songs around the piano,
Mum playing in the gloom,
Of candlelight and happy voices,
Echoing round the room.
Taking the dog for a swim at Exning,
Or up on Newmarket Heath.

Post office staff concerts,
For the workhouse folk 'neath
The rich and famous visiting,
For a few hours' view,
Of racing horses on the Rowley Mile,
Or exercising in the dew.

Dancing in the village halls,
To brother Charles' band.
A coach load of young people,
Yes, life was grand.
Then came the war, and off we went,
In khaki and in blue.

Life was never the same again,
We lost pals good and true.
But we married, had our children,
Now they are married too.
But our grandchildren will never know,
The old Newmarket that we knew.

Doreen Bacon

Childhood Dreams

Those halcyon paths we used to walk
Can only belong to our childhood
These paths we walk now are not hard and long
The rhythm is different as we sing the new song

My old toys are broken and torn
And my skates and bike rusty and worn
But my real car now is chromium clean
All the bright paintwork honed to a sheen

Cowboys and Indians, kings and queens
All the knocks and bruises led to tears in streams
Our tears now came when you were born
A new era of our lives rich and warm

Where does childhood end and adulthood begin
When do the games become serious and tempers thin
Do we really grow away from times forgotten?
Perhaps the memory fades as the years pass on

Because these are now our halcyon days

Colin Skilton

My Time

O to be young again, bursting with energy
When I thought I was the cat's whiskers
Playing three games of football in the same day
And badminton till the early hours
Cycling to my work every morn
Where did I get the time for courting?
The only time my mother saw me
Was when I appeared to be fed
And stumbled up the stairs to bed
If only I could have bottled the stamina
I could do with some of it now
I laughed when some of my elders
Told me that life was very short
Now I can tell the weather
With all my aches and pains
Now in my eighth decade
I realise how lucky I have been
To have had a loving wife and family
To cherish in my old age
If only I could turn the page
And start all over again
With the experience that I have now
Would I make less mistakes?
And be a much nicer person
Avoiding the vulnerability of youth
Clutching at straws in the wind
And thank God for my youth
With an old head on young shoulders.

Jim Rodger

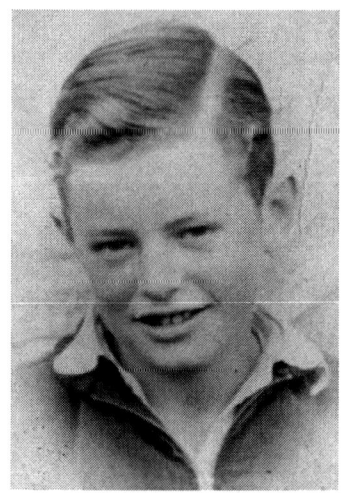

I Wish

Oh how I wish I was young again
To go for a walk down a country lane
Wander through fields so fresh and green
But I don't suppose you know what I mean.
Where once were fields, rows of houses stand
They have built on every little bit of land
Cars race along the motorways
Gone are the lazy summer's days.
Where a horse and cart would rumble along
And birds in the trees would be singing a song.
The children used to go out to play
Not sit indoors watching telly all day.
I could have ran for miles and miles
Happy and cheerful, a face full of smiles,
But that was such a long time ago
And now I am old the time does fly so.
I can't walk very far, my legs would give out,
But where would I go? With no country about.
If the world changes in the next eighty years
How it's altered for me, I have many fears
For our children's lives and the whole human race
If things continue to advance at this terrible pace
What faces them all in the years ahead
But why should I worry, I shall be dead.

Gladys Baillie

The Enemy

There is an enemy so bold
Who seeks a greater loot than gold.
He enters in by the front door,
And robs us of infinitely more.
He's snatched away a sable hair
And left a snowy white one there.
Skin's smoothness is a favourite prize,
He signs his theft around our eyes.
He spirits away our supple grace,
Leaving stiffness and pain in its place.
The vampire's thirst is satisfied
By the supply of our strength's tide.
As minutes tick by into hours
So drop by drop he sucks our powers
A strong, sweet voice, clear as a bell,
An ear that faintest sound could tell,
An eye so keen, that saw so far
And brighter shone than any star.
So on our life with indifference bland
He lays his with'ring, blighting hand.
Thus he robs us theft upon theft
Until we've very little left.
One treasure is beyond his grasp -
The Christ that in our hearts we clasp,
For what can sever from His love,
Or things below or things above?
Why should we grieve for earthly loss
If we are standing by His cross
And if upon Heaven our hopes are hung
Where we shall be forever young?

V M Archer

Childhood

When I was a little girl, I believed in angels, fairies and Santa Claus.
I still do.
I used to dream of finding the end of the rainbow and the crock of gold.
I searched for four leaf clovers to bring me luck.
My children believed in angels, fairies and Santa Claus.
They still do.
And when they asked me, 'Is Santa real?' I told them he was a symbol
they could see, for the feeling of happiness and giving that people
express for each other at Christmas time.
One November night when the air was crisp and frosty and the stars
were clear as crystals overhead, I woke them from their beds, wrapped
them in warm coats and boots and I took them into the garden to
experience with me what I had shared with my dad when I was young.
This was later reinforced by a visit to the planetarium.
They still remember.

Now I take my grandchildren to the bottom of the garden
to look for fairies.

Gwendoline Bennett

Groovy, Swingin' And Fab

Do they mean anything to you?
Twist and shake, the hitch hike too,
Do you remember those hot pants?
Getting an admiring glance,
'Shakin' it down' at a dance,
If flowers and bell, round a neck,
Caused a stir, what the heck!
'Slacks' worn low on the hips.
The black eyeliner and white lips,
Skinny rib' jumpers worn so tight!
Bell-bottomed jeans, looked so right.

'Peace and love', hippies would sing,
'Flower power' the *in* thing,
Do you remember nineteen sixty-nine?
'Make love not war, peace to mankind'
Bright beams of coloured strobe,
'Mods' and 'rockers' on scooters rode!
Then, modern version of a 'pony tail',
The hairstyle for male or female,
Hair, multicoloured blonde and black,
Worn loose and wild down a back!

The 'pop' song called 'Little Town Flirt'
High legged boots and the 'mini' skirt,
Did you wear them for a while,
Shoes or boots, platform style?
About morals, were different views,
Mary Quant fashion the in news,
Happy days, few were sad,
Some of the best ever had,
Daring, exciting, completely mad!
They were never really bad,
Those memories 'swingin', groovy and fab'.

Sheila Walters

Now And Then

Once I was young, now I'm old,
Once I was shy, now I am bold.
Once I was slim, now I'm fat,
Once I could see, now blind as a bat,
Once I could work all day long,
Now I am weak, once I was strong.
Once I could run and win a race,
Now my life is a much slower pace.
Once I had a good head of hair,
Now I am bald and I shed a tear.
A full set of teeth I had once,
Now I am gummy, can't eat my lunch.
Now I am old and wish I was young,
But that's no reason to be so glum.
Once I was young, now I am old,
Memories are worth their weight in gold.

Zoiyar

When Life Was Fun

Very nearly everything that happened
In those early days was fun to me.
My life was full of happy times and laughter
In complete security.

But soon bereavement struck; dark clouds which I'd not
Known existed, hid the sun.
My life became beset by fears and problems -
Though, of course, there still was fun.

Oh how I thank my God for friends and family
Who surrounded me with prayer.
Too young was I to understand at that time,
Endless depth of God's wise care.

Years later, though, I realised and I thanked Him
That His love triumphed again.
And now I praise Him for each step He's led me
All through life's fun, joy and pain.

Elma Heath

My Teenage Years

My teenage years
Where did they fly
Where curls were in
And skirts were wide
With stiffened petticoats that flounced
Then as you walked
Made skirts just bounce
Where belts would pull
Your waist in tight
With youth club dances
Each Saturday night
There was so much fun
With your friends of the day
You worked for little
But that was the way
I have seen many changes
Been through good and bad
The young days were some
Of the best that I've had

Jeanette Gaffney

The Good Old Days

Remember all those summer days,
   the birds, the bees, the flowers.
The service in the village church,
   - the sermon seemed like hours!

Remember all those holidays,
   the sand, the sea, the sky,
and running down the garden path
   to watch the trains go by.

Remember when we walked to school,
   or caught the ancient bus.
And all our pals and friends for life,
   and aunts who made a fuss.

Remember all the winter snow,
   the games and all the toys.
And Christmas time with Mum and Dad
   and laughing girls and boys.

O, how it seems so long ago
   when we were young and free,
but now we're all so old and slow
   just please remember me!

John Thorpe

Treasure Hunt

Curio shops with second-hand ware
Tales could be told by the goods being sold
Now relics of so long ago, once someone's treasures
Surplus now, to be sold.
Did that picture really hang on someone's wall?
The proud grandfather clock, tick quietly in a hall?
Memories of a past when things were made to last,
Cake stands for afternoon tea now you rarely see
Do pass the seed cake if you please
Boxes of nick-nacks, hat pins - tie pins, buckles off shoes.
Photos - who's who?
China, some never seeing light of day,
Stored in cabinets, so not to crack
Lots of memories - heartaches too
In curios of a bygone age
Like a book, page after page.

Margaret Parnell

The Picture

I carry a picture in my mind from many years ago
For sadly I was such a fool, of that I surely know
The things that seemed to matter then are not important now
My life has changed so very much I'm pleased to say - and how

My little girl was very small - no more than two or three
And all she wanted, bless her heart, was just to be with me
But though I loved her I was blind to everything but sport
I never gave her of myself the way I know I ought.

Now in my mind I still can see her, sobbing at the door
As I went off to play my game - a truly selfish bore
Oh! How I wish that I could turn the clock back all those years
I'd tell her how I loved her and I'd kiss away those tears.

I won a lot of trophies at whatever game I played
I felt quite proud and showed them off in cabinets displayed
Then I became a Christian and my values changed a lot
I soon began to realise I'd been a stupid clot.

Those cups and medals, badges, caps, I once admired so oft
I put them in a plastic bag and stuck them in the loft
They've been up there a long time now to tell the truth I find
I've more important things to do to occupy my mind.

There's one thing I must tell you now I'm very glad to say
My little girl was first to find that Jesus is the way
From early age all through the years each faithful prayer she sends
To God through Jesus every day, for family and friends.

She's married to a fine young man - they have two lovely boys
God's called him to evangelise - it's work that he enjoys
They complement each other for they're both of one accord
And pulling all together they're a powerhouse for the Lord.

Keith Johnson

Then And Now

When we were young we had all the future,
And time lay untarnished in her crystal glass;
But as we surrender to time's mortal nature,
We find we increasingly have just the past.

Oh when we were young we did all the dreaming,
And life lay uncovered in her secret room;
But subject to fickle old age's scheming,
We venture another day nearer the tomb.

When youth was gifted, we had all the passion,
The fire and the danger and wildness of joy;
But as we grow older, we give up the fashion
Of anger, and mellow to be broken toys.

Oh when life was singing her song of seduction,
And luring us onward and evermore on,
We little then guessed that our powers of deduction
Would fade and then falter, and then be quite gone.

But now time has tarnished and brought disillusion,
And all of our brave dreams have floundered and drowned.
Life has betrayed us, and left us confusion,
And age leads us sadly to lie underground.

Anne Rolfe-Brooker

Halcyon

There were fish in the sea and the fire of youth
Anybody not your age was old,
Unheeded advice that strangled the truth
So it seemed that you were told.

But time tells a story that cannot hide
As the ebb and the flows of the tide,
Which once was now, is then.

John M Heddle

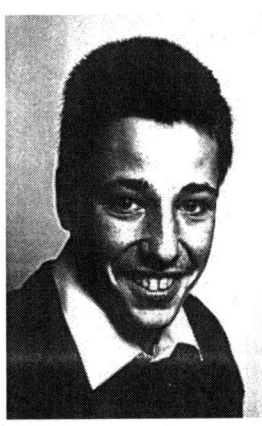

Memories

I have many memories,
Both bad and good,
Of playing on the Isle of Wight,
Where the sun is very bright.
I have memories of building sandcastles,
By the sea.
I have memories of opening Christmas presents and parcels
And memories of the birth of my cousins, Jay and Chloe.
Everyone has memories of various decades;
The 1960s gave people memories
Of teddy boys, bunny girls and Twiggy.
The 1940s gave people memories
Of seeing their homes turn to dust,
Of their husbands going off to fight,
Children and their mates
Getting on a train
To the countryside,
Away from their mothers
And fathers,
They might never see again.
I have memories of buying a mobile phone,
And of visiting the Millennium Dome.
A memory is a powerful thing.
Some have memories of when they first heard Elvis sing.
Everyone has memories
Special and important to them,
And I other memories,
Special, important and personal,
Only to me.

Jason Pointing

Broken Playgrounds

I sit beside my friend
until I go to bed,
just because I cannot speak
they treat me like I'm dead.
I hear the words they speak
around me as I lay
and pray that with the morrow
they'll hear the words I say.
I'd love to tell of happiness
that I had years ago
of the man I found to love
and how he loved me so.
I'm not really past it
just because I'm grey and old,
my mind plays in the playground
of the young and of the bold.
For no one can take from me
the memories that I keep
and if they will not hear me
then I will keep them deep.
But one day maybe someone
will look me in the eye
and see the spark I'm carrying
with me till I die.

Brenda Weir

Old Folk

Here I sit with the Old Folk
Amongst ale an' smoke
An' each 'as a story
'Bout youngsters in glory

The dialect broad an' cheery
Does make our chins beery
Days of fishing -
An' near been missing

But it never gets too black
An' we're soon back
To Aunty Mave's knitting
An' how it's never fitting

The crackle of a well-lit fire
An' the sound of that ol' Spitfire
All at the bottom of our glass
Just finishing our last

Rosy-cheeked an' grinning
Not a glass to be seen brimming
An' now we're ready for bed
For all our yesterdays have been said!

R E Bonsor

Untitled

I often sit and reminisce,
About the old times that I miss.
Smoking chimney, cobbled street,
Sparking clogs 'neath my feet.
Dancing nightly with my beau,
Doing the twist 'go man go'!

Mary Lawson

The Playground

With an allocated area for football,
played with soft balls, real footballs
bouncing on tarmac, being kicked
so aggressively, broke school windows.

He wanted to be picked by the big boys
to play in either the up or the down side.
They said, he wasn't good enough.

They let him be a spectator providing
he stood, so he also acted as a goal post.
'Watch and learn,' they added, knowingly.

He preferred to think of himself
as the coach or referee, depending
on the current state of play.

These self-appointed positions
ended in a loss of face and tears.
As a coach he was ignored.

The foul he spotted as a referee
resulted in a penalty, the ball
placed on a disputed nine yard spot.
When finally kicked, hit him in the face.

'Hard luck, you hit the post,' they shouted.
He retrieved the ball, attended to his bloody nose,
returned determined to be more diligent.

Les Merton

The Passage Of Time

My oh my, how times have changed
Many say for the better but that depends
So much is now streamlined and so very sterile
Food must be consumed by a certain date or there is peril
Almost everybody's attitude has gone awry
Those old-fashioned courtesies do not now apply
So many appear selfish as they clamour on the way
They have no time, always rushing to bid the time of day

Yes, perhaps years ago we lived a slower pace
Folk seemed more concerned if they had not seen your face
Neighbours would come knocking and enquire if all was well
Older folk felt more comfortable but now neglect is sheer hell
So much grief and hardship in this so-called modern world
Many rules and regulations and of those many are absurd
Converting to the metric system goes against the grain
Surely we are English and English measurements should remain

A multicultural society, we all try to do our best
It's so difficult at times as we are often put to the test
How life was lived, alas we cannot compare as we attempt to guide
New introductions that please some whilst others cannot abide
Standing back and taking stock, has this life been a bore?
When we were young many fought the Hun in a cruel and bloody war
Today we attempt to live in peace if those agitators let us
Sealing the wounds of disbelief to improve our life in faith and trust

R D Hiscoke

Time Marches On

In the early morning of life
The sands through the Hourglass of Time
Do so slowly seem to flow:
Energy levels are high; tasks are few
Thus Time is that delay waiting for:
That next meal of the day
That next chance with friends to play

By late morning
learning has occupied our time
In preparation
for our adult role
And in the expectation
Of having with another
A loving and rewarding
Inter relation

The early afternoon sees a task escalation
Family responsibilities are now our lot
And tasks now take a toll of time
And energy levels suffer quite a drop
'Tis then a glimpse is caught of that upland green
From where the chains of care are shed
And where a loving mother and wife
May now - at long last - relax instead

'Tis now the evening of life
The loved one is lost
Energy levels are low
Tasks fill the time left
For those who are bereft
Time marches on - regardless

V W Lown

Flying By Day

Flying by day,
Jiving by night,
We laughed and cried together.
When work was done
And weariness gone
Our spirits grew high
And tiredness, flew, into the sky.

June Fletcher

That Girl In The Dress

Where did she get to, that girl in the dress?
Who has she been down the years?
Has she had happiness - laughter - success?
Or has there been nothing but tears?

What has she done with her life since that day -
When she smiled for the camera - happy to say
'Look out world - where's the fun?
Here I come - twenty-one!'

Africa beckoned her - just for a year -
And deserts were crossed (she'd no fear).
Adventures were frequent - relationships strong,
But, with travelling around, never long.

Where did she think she'd be living, when old?
Who did she hope she would be?
Did she intend to be somebody's wife -
In a bungalow, down by the sea?

Is she quite happy with what she's achieved?
Her career? (Cut off short by her girls -
But she never resented the staying at home to look after them -
Never felt peeved!)

She looks to her future - career now resumed,
But retirement's not *that* far away.
She still has ambitions - they're not quite the same,
And she sometimes just lives for the day!

She looks in the mirror and who does she see?
Someone different who's now fifty-three.
She takes a hard look at the face that looks back,
And she asks herself - can that be me?

Bits of her now aren't quite in the same place,
And the wrinkles do show in her face!
But she looks in the mirror and what does she find?
She is still twenty-one in her mind!

Irene Jones

Growing Old

I'm growing old disgracefully
A rum and Coke I must agree
Does more for me than a cup of tea
And I don't care what becomes of me
Growing old disgracefully!

I'm growing old disgracefully
Flirting with the girls I see
Taking Viagra with my tea
Or going on a gambling spree
Growing old disgracefully!

I'm growing old disgracefully
Still footloose and fancy free
A dolly bird upon each knee
Oh what fun it is to be
Growing old disgracefully!

Fred Magan

Then And Now

Then, I was slender, light as a feather,
Now, I am pretty well built, let's say
Now, I enjoy a daytime siesta
Then, I could dance the night away

The girl that I was, still lingers within
The woman I was to become
The shyness still there,
And can still overwhelm
In moments of despair

There have been plenty of those in my life
But plenty of joys as well
The 'ups and downs'
The rough with the smooth
The future, who can foretell?

To be a 'whole' person embraces a spectrum
A walk of faith, with fears
Mountains and molehills
An aerial view, with exaltations
Interspersed with vales of frustrations and tears.

I can still summon up the hesitant child
Whose nose was pressed against the windowpane
Who peeped from behind the scenes,
From behind the skirts of her mother,
But I can't vacillate in adult life
It causes too much bother

Fate demands a more interactive role
Than to stay behind the windowpane
In everyday struggles, the courage is given
The wisdom, the patience, the firmness of purpose
The heat to withstand, yet firm remain.

Beryl Moorehead

Lifetime

Then, I was unaware of responsibility
Now it is a burden.
Then, time could stand still
Now it flies so fast.
Then I thought grown-ups knew everything
Now I know they don't.
Then there was so much to learn
Now there still is.
Then I thought I knew best
Now I'm sure of nothing.
Then my head was full of dreams
Now I know dreams rarely come true.
Then I was just a little girl, a child
Now I'm a mother and a grandmother.
I've had many blessings, many heartaches
One blessing is, I can remember now, how I felt then.
One heartache, the world's so full of sin.
We will never learn.
What are we teaching our children?
We could do so much better as a world
Couldn't we?

A Heathershaw

ANCHOR BOOKS SUBMISSIONS INVITED
SOMETHING FOR EVERYONE

ANCHOR BOOKS GEN - Any subject,
light-hearted clean fun, nothing unprintable please.

THE OPPOSITE SEX - Have your say on the opposite gender. Do
they drive you mad or can we co-exist in harmony?

THE NATURAL WORLD - Are we destroying the world around
us? What should we do to preserve the beauty and the future of our
planet - you decide!

All poems no longer than 30 lines.
Always welcome! No fee!
Plus cash prizes to be won!

Mark your envelope (eg *The Natural World)* And send to:
Anchor Books
Remus House, Coltsfoot Drive
Peterborough, PE2 9JX

OVER £10,000 IN POETRY PRIZES
TO BE WON!

Send an SAE for details on our New Year 2002 competition!